This book is dedicated to the teachers who should still be teaching.

Bad School Leadership
(and what to do about it)

By Omar Akbar

Contents

Introduction

A little bit about me

I've been a full-time science teacher for 13 years across 4 different schools. My passion is very much for the classroom - I was once even nominated for a teacher award – but I have never wanted to become a middle or senior leader. I have, however, taken similar responsibilities for things like student leadership, eco-schools, and mentoring PGCEs and NQTs. I never went further because anything related to data, spreadsheets, or otherwise involving a lot of deskwork, doesn't really appeal to me.

I choose to be happy a teacher most of the time. In addition to keeping my diet, exercise, sleep and relationships as a priority, over the years I've learnt to compartmentalise and focus my energy on the things that make the job worth it. Like the basketball match we just had against our year 9s, or the time I asked my year 10s 'Any questions?' and someone put their hand up and asked, 'How old were you when you started going bald, Sir?' And, of course, the results days upon which many of my pupils thank me for having taught them. Teaching really can be the best job ever.

I'm by no means a poster boy for teacher happiness. The high workload, bureaucracy, stress, and, on one occasion, workplace bullying, has got to me on a handful of occasions over the years. During these times – much like many of you may have done – I considered working abroad. But, at this point in my life, I can quite comfortably say that, if I were I to do this, it would only really be to escape the English weather and the short daylight hours over winter. If only neither of these were factors affecting wellbeing!

Having taught in 4 schools, having been a union rep, and from the success of my first book *The (Un)official Teacher's Manual: What they don't teach you in training*, I have developed a vast network from which I have had the opportunity to hear a lot of teachers' experiences, good and bad. Two things stand out: school leadership varies drastically across the country and, in the case of the school leaders who aren't getting it right, it's the same things they're getting wrong. At least they're consistent across the board.

The teaching crisis

18% of teachers plan to leave the profession within 2 years.[1]

30% of teachers who qualified in 2010 quit the state sector within 5 years of qualifying.[2]

54% of teachers report poor mental health.[3]

80% of teachers have seriously considered leaving the profession in the last 12 months.[4]

4 out of 5 teachers have experienced workplace bullying in the last year.[5]

55% of teachers would not recommend a career in teaching.[6]

In other words, too many teachers are miserable. A significant proportion of us are statistically likely to leave the profession; develop mental health issues, get bullied, or in the most serious cases all the above. Fills you with joy, doesn't it?

Not about the system

The aforementioned statistics are *partly* an unfortunate by-product of the education system itself, in that they are partially caused by external factors over which school leaders have limited or no control. This book is not about the system, at least not that part of it. As you read, you'll notice that I've made no mention of the fact that if you were to ask 5 teachers at your school what a 'current grade' is, you'd probably get 5 different answers. I've made no mention of the fact that if you were to ask 5 teachers at your school how they arrived at their 'forecast' or 'expected' grades, you'd get 10 different answers. I've made no mention of how we're almost never allowed to give a child a grade on a data point lower than the grade from the previous data point, even if they've since underperformed. I've made no mention of the need to follow a marking policy. I've made no mention of how school leaders pull pupils out of subjects they like and are good at, to put them into subjects they don't like and are bad at, in a bid to keep the school's progress 8 scores high. All of these things cause stress, confusion and dismay, but school leaders aren't entirely responsible.

Before you begin

This book is about the management – or rather, the mismanagement – of the system, the factors over which school leaders do have full control. While school leaders aren't entirely responsible, they play a role in the teaching crisis, so it makes sense to discuss what is being done wrong (What Went Wrong) and suggest areas for improvement (Even Better If) for school leaders as they are still a key determinant of a teacher's happiness. I ask that, as you read, you bear in mind 3 things: firstly, as mentioned earlier, school leadership varies drastically across the country, so avoid making generalisations. Secondly, just because a school leader does a couple of the things I write about, it doesn't make them entirely bad. It's all relative, but the more things you can relate to in here, the more likely it is that your school is a toxic one. Thirdly, there are lots of good school leaders, as you'll see!

As well as suggesting areas for improvement for school leaders, I'll also discuss the ways in which we, the teachers, can influence our leaders. For those of you who have read my first book, you'll notice that the advice in there is very 'play it safe.' The reason for that is because I didn't want, to put it bluntly, new teachers walking around with a target on their head. In the second part of this book, you'll come across some advice that doesn't necessarily follow the same ethos. The reason for this is because this advice is for *all* teachers, rather than *individual* teachers and if *everyone* acts upon it, not only will it be highly effective, it will also be risk free.

As ranting about SLTs can be so much fun, I've injected some hyperbole for your amusement.
Enjoy the read, and teachers, for your sake, I hope there's not a single WWW example that you can relate to. Good school leaders, you already know that a happy teacher is

a good teacher. For you, I hope the EBI examples are just stating the obvious.

1.

Relationship building

Relationship building

Somewhere between the time when Blondie told us to call her and Rick Astley told us he'd never give us up, it all began: In the 1980s, bosses bossed. Emotional intelligence was voluntarily forfeited, and employees were talked down to by intimidating bosses. There was no carrot, just a stick, with which rigorous accountability measures were enforced. The motivational movies of the time (*The Karate Kid, Rocky*) probably became popular because everyone's spirit was crushed from the metaphoric butt-kicking.

Most industries, including ours, eventually realised the inefficacy of this approach and – along with the big earrings and mullets – threw most of it out. However, perhaps more often than should be the case, some schools seem to be stuck in the past and school leaders are not doing the one thing that could make their school successful by all measures: they are not building relationships with their staff.

Leading through influence is more effective than leading through authority, and nowhere is this truer than in schools. Teachers are warming up to, and therefore more likely to embrace, the ideas of a leader with whom they have a good relationship. How are these relationships built? Well, it's the not-so-little, little things.

Empathy

Apparently 1 in 25 of us is a sociopath. This means that one pupil per class and between 1 and 9 teachers per school do not have any empathy to speak of. Scary thought. But no matter how bad your SLT, there is a good chance your school governors didn't deliberately seek to monopolise the country's best sociopaths – even though it may feel like it! Bad school leaders make the monumental error of shutting down empathy *deliberately.*

Isn't it funny how we light up when we see a funny (often relevant) teaching meme? You'll notice too, that many of the memes are to do with the less desirable aspects of the job, but as well as making us laugh, the empathic creator has spelt out exactly how we feel and in doing so has made those aspects more bearable. Almost bitter-sweet.

In subtle and unsubtle ways, good school leaders will create an empathic ethos. The Headteacher may tell parents who arrive late to leave once parents' evening is over, or may joke about how they hope there's another snow day on Friday during a Thursday briefing. They may be completely understanding when your results weren't as good as they were last year or (as I once experienced) they may give you a lift all the way home in the snow when the buses aren't running. I remember in my NQT year when, after I received some sad news, the Deputy Head came to see me and told me if I didn't feel able to teach that day I could go home. The mere fact that he asked was enough to give me the will to finish the school day.

Communication

Anyone who's studied for a PGCE would have been told two things thousands of times: firstly, most communication is non-verbal and secondly, the way we say things is more important than what we say, (at least if we are looking for a desired response).

One would think then that good communication skills would be a prerequisite to school leadership! Sadly, however, too often are we told of school leaders who shout, belittle and publicly chastise. And if verbal aggression wasn't enough, how's this for a *non*-verbal aggression? At one school, staff briefing began at 8.35am. SLT would not arrive until 8.40am and, when they did, all 12 of them would stand in a big line at the front of the staffroom and await silence. Some staff got fed of up this deliberate display of authority and decided to follow suit and arrive 8.40am. SLT actually had the cheek to tell them off for arriving late to briefing.

Effective school leaders, while maintaining a professional distance, remain part of the crowd. They smile, they make eye contact, they make small talk and, most importantly, they never speak or otherwise act in such a way that would make their staff feel like subordinates. Before data generating, spreadsheet making, curriculum updating or any other skill, an aspiring school leader should master the art of being personable. We teachers are constantly working against many factors out of our control; what we need is to know and feel that our leaders are on the same side as us. Not just there to watch us and tell us what to do.

Sense of humour

I spoke to a Headteacher a while back who told me that he put the following question on the list when interviewing for teaching staff: what is the most important quality a teacher must have? He was looking neither for resilience, good organisation or even passion. The answer he wanted was 'a good sense of humour.' He didn't deem other answers to be wrong, but to him, the absence of this quality meant that other qualities were less compelling.

On good days, we laugh and on bad days, if we don't laugh, we'll cry. As teachers, we know the importance of a sense of humour very well. But there is no reason for it to stop in the classroom.

'Sky News, BBC, or CNN. I could have told any of them...but it was easier just to tell Mr. Smith.' was how one Deputy Head confirmed the rumours that he would indeed be leaving, one morning briefing.

Another, after announcing that sniffer dogs would be visiting the school, sarcastically told staff that they should leave their marijuana at home because dogs can't distinguish between pupils and teachers! It's not the only reason, but staff are markedly happier in schools where leaders have an overtly good sense of humour.

Everyone can win

Much of what has been discussed so far, falls under the general umbrella of emotional intelligence: the capacity to be aware of, control, and express one's emotions, and to handle interpersonal relationships judiciously and empathetically. Emotional Intelligence is at the heart, then, of relationship building. But why are relationships so important?

Teaching is a job that is high in what psychologists refer to as 'emotional labour', the process of managing feelings and expressions to fulfil the emotional requirements of a job. When added to the hours of triple marking, the low-level disruption and the intense accountability, an emotionally unintelligent boss will worsen the problem, probably more than they would in other professions. School leaders who build positive relationships with their teachers therefore ease, rather than add to, the aforementioned emotional labour.

I very much doubt anyone ever enrolled on a PGCE thinking '*I can't wait to be a school leader one day so I can humiliate teachers!*' Of course not. Often bad school leaders lead the way they do due to external pressures and the unreasonable accountability measures placed on them. From this, they either develop the warped belief that it is not possible to do 'what's best for the kids' and still have happy teachers, or they believe – rightly or wrongly – that people will do more to avoid pain than they will to gain pleasure, and so adapt a harsh approach. Some, of course, are just disagreeable people.

It may work in the short term (people will do anything at gun point) but the alarming statistics strongly indicate that it's not sustainable. For many teachers, pain breaks them: It makes them cry in the car on the way home. It makes them cry at school. It makes them have thoughts they'd never share with their loved ones. It gives them anxiety attacks. It makes them contemplate crashing their car on the way to work. It makes them tell everyone to never apply to the school they work at. It makes them look for jobs abroad. It makes them leave the profession.

On a positive note, much of this is entirely under the control of school leaders. Praise your staff and they will feel valued and work harder. Show empathy toward your staff and they will invest in you because they know you're invested in them. Use humour with your staff and they will better trust you. Properly respond to their emotional state and they will respect you.

By adapting the wrong leadership strategies, we are also potentially harming our children. In 2019, research showed that stress passed from teachers to pupils 'like a contagion'.[7] A stressed teacher means a stressed pupil and stressed pupils don't learn. Children deserve a teacher who is present in the moment, focused solely on them. Not one who's in a perpetual state of worry.

So leaders: just stop it. Be like the Deputy Head who once took 3 piles of books off a teary NQT when she saw her in the car park on a Friday evening. Be like the Headteacher who took a pot of stew to a Head of Department's house when he was off with stress and told him to take as long as he needed. Be like the Assistant Head who didn't copy 5 people into an email when a teacher accidentally missed out the current grades on his year 8 reports. Be emotionally intelligent. Everyone will win.

2.

Observations

Observations

Lesson observations are a common source of stress for many teachers. The unnerving feeling of being watched, the potential consequences of a poor lesson and the sheer number of human variables over which a teacher has limited control are enough to put many teachers on edge. But, as there are very few industries in which an employee is neither monitored nor scrutinised, some of this is – and may always be – part and parcel of our job.

The problem, however, is not the observation itself: It is the way in which it is done and the implications thereof.

WWW: 'Do what you normally do. We're not trying to catch you out.' – SLT

Don't get me wrong, if SLT say this, mean it and practice it, then it's not an issue. In fact, it's actually beneficial for staff wellbeing to create a relaxed climate as opposed to a climate of fear. What's going wrong, however, is that sometimes, the above is just not true.

Not too long ago, teachers took to twitter with the '#nobservation' hashtag to describe some of their observation experiences. Not all experiences of course, but just the ones which can only really be described as, well, ludicrous. Take a look. The purpose of the 'n' will become very clear!

David Cummins@Cummins86

My #nobservation told me my jumper was too similar to the school uniform and I need to stand out. I'm a 6ft tall man at a girls' school.

Mrs Coster@miss_coster

Told my lesson was RI once, when I asked for feedback on how to improve the response was 'book your observation in earlier because we had already hit our quota of good teachers before we made it to you!'

Clare Round@Curliclare

#nobservation I got told my lesson would have been outstanding if I had removed a dead plant from the back of the classroom.

Ian Addison@ianaddison

#nobservation was picked up on the fact that i hadn't used lollysticks to randomly select pupils for questioning and this was bad afl. Next obs i used (blank) sticks and still just asked the children i wanted to ask.

Fay@_Zooks

I was told after an observation that (while all the outstanding criteria had been ticked off on feedback sheet) it wasn't outstanding because 'I just didn't have that feeling.' #NOBservation

Carl Rogers@_CarlRogers_

First obs at a NEW school:

'Your lesson was RI. It was great but if any aspect of your lesson was RI, then that's the overall judgement. The planning format that you used is RI.'

THE SCHOOL'S OWN FORMAT!

Now it's true that many people may embellish or exaggerate, particularly on social media. The desire for 'likes', the desire to self-promote or the desire to have a laugh sometimes get the better of us and we post things which may not be so accurate. In the case of the #nobservation tweets however, I believe their proof is in their resonance. The fact that so many teachers could relate is testimony to their truth.

#Nobservation aside, there can be a substantial disconnect between what school leaders *say* they are doing and what they are actually doing: Most teachers can speak of some inane, pesky or pernickety feedback they've received. If dead plants are being mentioned in your observation then, yes, they *are* trying to catch you out, no matter how much they may say otherwise.

EBI: You stopped being so annoying

If you had to dig deep to think of a suggestion with which to improve a teacher's lesson, then yes, you guessed it: you probably shouldn't have mentioned it. All you've done is annoyed the teacher and possibly caused a feeling of disillusionment which could easily have been avoided had you kept your big mouth shut. You may be desperate to make yourself look diligent, but being anal has no positive purpose in the long run. Let a teacher use whatever font they want to in their Power Points and remember that a dead plant has never harmed anyone.

Jokes aside, what you should do is focus on the positives and make sure a good teacher walks away smiling with the knowledge that they are valued. Make a point of bigging up the positives and don't lose your sense of proportion when suggesting areas for development. Appreciated teachers are happier teachers and happier teachers are more productive teachers. It's the pupils that ultimately benefit.

WWW: 'Support' plans

I don't think any of us will debate the fact that if a teacher is not quite getting it right, then they should be offered support in the first instance. If after having been sufficiently supported they still aren't progressing, then unfortunately it can only go one way. Inherently, support plans are not a negative – they are a positive necessity. Issues arise however, when support plans become 'support' plans.

Some schools have either a knee jerk or an outright aggressive reaction to a bad lesson observation. School leaders will ignore a teacher's track record of good observations, and more importantly, their daily good practice and make them feel wholly inadequate by placing them on a 'support' plan after one bad observation. The anxiety caused by the constant meetings, observations, learning walks, and action plans are enough to begin an otherwise good teachers downward spiral. In the worst case (but not-so-uncommon) scenario, the teacher's confidence becomes ruined beyond repair and they leave the school, or sadly, the profession. This is destructive, not supportive.

EBI: Let the teacher speak

After an observation every teacher's most loved and hated question usually follows: 'How do you think it went?'

If you've just observed a lesson which wasn't too good, this is the best time to allow the teacher to speak. Having had the skill of reflection drummed into us since our teacher training days, most of us can tell you exactly what went wrong and how we would improve it were we to do it again. Give the teacher the benefit of the doubt and assume they can do this. Why? Because this way it'll save you both a lot of bother: If they've acknowledged their lesson could've gone a lot better, then you don't have to go through the headache involved in the aftermath. Some school leaders will sit (and almost passionately) list the negatives of the lesson until the teacher is reduced to tears, despite the teacher *knowing* it wasn't their best. Just ask them when they want to be re-observed and leave it that. Make sure they walk away smiling.

The only time some kind of support is necessary is when there is a considerable disconnect between your judgement and the teachers. Please note, 'considerable' is the operative word here: there can and should be healthy debate during feedback which should not lead to some damning form of 'support.'

Back in the days of lesson grading (which by the way, should no longer be taking place), my lesson was graded as a 3, or 'requires improvement', by a senior leader for some inane reason. During the feedback I was admittedly irate and stormed out the room as I knew it was a solid grade 2. I complained to the Headteacher whose exact words to the best of my memory were: 'You've done a phenomenal job since you started. Observations are a judgement call and what one would observer would grade as a 3, another would grade as a 2.' She didn't even insist on a re-observation, let alone a support plan. That's good leadership. On another note, while I got up to storm out the room, somehow my apple flew out of my sandwich box, so after storming out, I had to storm back in again and pick it up from under the observer's chair.

WWW: My way or the highway

While most schools' observation criteria overlap as they follow their interpretation of what is given to them by Ofsted, some schools tend to try and 'out Ofsted' Ofsted. In a bid to be stricter than the big 'O', they sneak in their own criteria under the guise of 'this is what Ofsted want to see,' when in reality they don't. For example, take a school that put a box with the phrase 'marking for impact' on the feedback sheet, in which observers had to put an individual grade, along with grades for behaviour, progress and so on. At the time, no such phrase was used in anything published by Ofsted, but a grade 3 in this box alone was enough to render the whole lesson a grade 3 – requires improvement. Making sure a teacher is following the marking policy is one thing, but if pupils' books still indicate that their target grade has not been reached, then surely the fault lies with whoever made the policy in the first place? In other words, if a teacher is following the marking policy and it is not making the desired impact, then the 'problem' lies outside the remit of the teacher. Practices such as these cause nothing but confusion and additional stress that could very easily be avoided.

EBI: Stick to the script

Whatever Ofsted want to see in lessons, has already been outlined by… wait for it…Ofsted. How strange? Adding to the criteria is, in my opinion, both unnecessary and unacceptable. If you want to see something else in a lesson, then *say* that it is *you* who wants to see it. Don't play the Ofsted card. Also, sorry to state the obvious, but surely if it's good enough for the government, it's good enough for your school? And let me save you some suspense: making your observations harsher or more obscure will not improve pupils' results. What it will do is make your staff browse the TES for jobs in their free periods because they don't understand why they're being asked to go above and beyond when they're already trying their hardest. Stick to the script.

WWW: Pupil voice

During lesson observations, observers often ask the pupils questions such as 'How is this lesson different from other lessons?', 'Are you sufficiently challenged in lessons?' and

'Is homework set regularly?' to name but a few. Like support plans, there is nothing inherently negative about pupil voice questions as pupils are often a good judge of a teacher. Anyone who's been off work for longer than a week knows that while pupils may initially be excited about the prospect of a supply teacher, the thrill soon turns into frustration. They want their favourite teacher back because they know they learn from them and, perhaps unconsciously, they know they need rules and boundaries.

The problems, in essence, come when pupil voice is not heard through an adult filter.

Take for example, the word 'boring.' When I teach ionic bonding, I teach it from the front with nothing but a board marker and my voice. I may get pupils to come to the front and draw examples or I may get them to draw the atoms on mini white boards. I may give them a worksheet in the last fifteen minutes of the lesson. They're engaged, they make substantial progress, but there's no real *excitement* in the traditional sense. If someone were to ask them if it was a fun lesson, I'm not too sure what they'd say. They might say it was boring as it's not exactly their first choice of entertainment, or they might say it was fun as I let them get away with making a 'bald' joke – nothing related to ionic bonding, but it still sticks with them. Depending on what exactly the observer asked the pupils and how it was interpreted, in my feedback I could quite easily be accused of being a boring teacher. At times, teachers find themselves on the defensive against such obscure accusations.

Observers also ask pupils about what they are learning in the observed lesson in a bid to measure the progress being made (because teachers can't do it themselves, right?). For many pupils, this is actually quite intimidating; they think that it is *them* under scrutiny. To react to this, pupils often say just enough for the observer to stop talking to them, for example, 'I don't know', or 'photosynthesis' (when the lesson was definitely about ionic bonding!). Again, during feedback, teachers will find themselves on the defence.

As some of us are driven by the need to tick and fill in boxes when there is genuinely nothing to put in them, we create things. Once the observer has asked the pupils a bunch of questions which they have answered 'correctly', for example, they may keep asking them questions until they get one wrong. The observer then puts whatever they said in the teacher's 'areas for development' box. This is as obvious as it is annoying and it's fair to say that no teacher will improve from feedback acquired in such a way.

In the most extreme cases, some observers will ask questions which are leading and have no other purpose but to enable teacher blaming. In one case, a Deputy Head sat next to an underachieving pupil and asked them 'Are you not meeting your target grade because Miss Smith isn't supporting you?' It's sad that this happens more often than you might think. For me, the consequences of this type of leadership are obvious.

EBI: You are the adult

Yes, some kids consider some teachers and some lessons boring. I just did my laundry, it was boring. I'm doing my grocery shopping later, that'll be boring. Everything's boring. You're boring, I'm boring, there are probably times when even Arnold Schwarzenegger is a bit of a drag to be around. Every time you speak during staff briefing teachers are bored. So bored that they fantasise about watching paint dry just to stay awake.

Ok. Ok. You're not that bad. But seriously, remove the word 'boring' from anything you ask a pupil. Replacing it with the word 'engaging' or 'interesting' would be far more effective and a lot less insulting to the teacher. Keep your questions simple like those described earlier, and don't go looking for dirt. It's pupil voice not a cross-examination so it shouldn't take longer than a few minutes. Realise also that there is the odd pupil who will use pupil voice as chance to get revenge on a teacher who they perceive to be a bit more stern, a bit less friendly or a bit more rigorous with sanctions than some of their colleagues.

If you ask pupils about that they're learning about, then do so with the knowledge that they may simply not want to talk to you or may struggle to verbalise concepts, particularly when put on the spot. I once taught ionic bonding (I can teach other topics, I promise!) to a top set year 11 group who would give long, rambling explanations with frequent pauses and hesitations when asked to verbally explain the concept. Diagrammatically, however, their answers were perfect. If you want happy, productive staff your approach must be holistic and your emotional intelligence should not go out the window when conducting pupil voice.

WWW: Too many observations

The frequency of lesson observations highlights some embarrassing inconsistencies across schools. While this is a problem when we *compare* schools rather than when we look *within* a school, it still warrants mentioning that some UK teachers may only be formally observed for 25 minutes a year, while others may be observed for an hour every 3 weeks. Both teachers nonetheless receive the same salary. Many senior leaders harp on about the importance of whole school consistency, but consistency between schools and within schools is equally as important if we want teachers to remain happy and in the profession.

A while back I was on an interview and another candidate told me that the reason he applied was because at his current school, he was observed every day. I remember looking at him with sheer disbelief and asking 'Surely you mean you get a daily drop-in?' 'No. I get observed *every day*.' Turns out his school's staff hierarchy was very top heavy, so SLT were on some crazy rota where every teacher had 25 mins of a lesson observed every day. Yes. Every. Day. Of course, such schools are utterly toxic, and this is the worst case scenario, but experienced staff still complain about being treated as trainees via their school's observation procedures.

What some SLTs seem to be voluntarily ignorant of is the fact that teachers talk. The inner workings of a school will be discussed with fellow teachers at other schools, so SLT run the risk of losing their existing staff or potential applicants to schools which have more professional trust. The retention crisis then worsens. In addition, some SLTs see observations as a way of getting rid of 'bad' teachers. If you're a good teacher, they argue, it shouldn't be a problem as you're just doing what you normally do. This logic is heavily flawed because even the best teachers don't want SLT, as a former colleague once put it, 'all up in their business.' To add insult to injury, SLT usually teach (depending on the school) anywhere between 2 and 12 lessons a week, so when *they* get observed, they don't experience the same intensity and hence some of them struggle to understand why observations are such a big deal.

EBI: Stop the obsession

Next time you and your fellow school leaders go on one of your fancy five-star hotel courses or conferences (Aspire to Inspire; Inspire to Aspire; Outstanding School Leadership; Leadership for Outstanding Schools; Managing Difficult Conversations; Successful Difficult Conversations; to name a few), why not agree to a limit on the number of observations a year? There is clear union guidance on this, so why not all agree to follow it, instead of doing whatever you can get away with? It's not that hard and it will do a lot for recruitment and retention. Teachers are more likely to teach where they are trusted as professionals and where there is significantly less hoop jumping.

Having said this, much of this suggestion is related to formal observations, as in the ones that in some way count towards performance management. Observations in themselves are not a bad thing and the process can actually be a good way to develop a teacher's practice. For example, in schools where teachers are happy, 'teachmeets' (where teachers exchange ideas and resources) are calendared into SIP days. Informal 'teaching buddy' observations are popular and formal observations are minimal. Sadly, some schools seem to fixate on wasting time and energy on monitoring rather than developing staff. Stop the obsession.

WWW: Who and when

Some school leaders tell their teachers in September the group or lesson they're being observed with in December, while others may tell you on Friday that you're being observed on Monday. Again, the inconsistency is alarming. How is it that someone who is forced to work over the weekend gets paid the same as someone who doesn't?

Within schools, rather than between schools then, where it's going wrong is that some SLTs think it's fashionable to say the classic line 'Do what you normally do. We're not trying to catch you out,' then take as much control away from the teacher as possible. They will choose the group (or lesson) you get observed with, the time you get observed, and they will give you as much or as little notice as they feel. What follows is this: one teacher gets a well-behaved top set year 11 on a Monday morning, and another gets observed with their rowdy year 9s on Friday period 5. One gets told how outstanding their lesson was, while the other gets told how much better their lesson could've been. Then, well, you know the rest.

The problem is that when the notice period is a short one, or the group or lesson has been dictated to you, it is difficult for some teachers to believe that SLT are looking for good practice. Rather, it suggests that they are looking for bad practice, they *are* trying to catch you out in a similar way to the peskiness described in the #nobservation tweets. Why? Because not a single teacher is on top of their marking all the time, or can teach every topic equally well, and we all know that, for some classes, a fight at lunch time or a wasp coming into the room is enough to completely ruin your lesson!

To cite a (thankfully) extreme case, there was a school which rather stupidly decided to make their performance management observations mirror an Ofsted inspection. In other words, they would tell you about your observation on the morning of the day before. Oh, and they wouldn't tell you the group or lesson either, so you had you had to write lesson plans for all of them. I wonder what their staff retention was like...

EBI: Stop the sneak attacks

If we want to make the profession more desirable, we must control the variables we *can* control, for the simple reason that too many variables are *out* of our control. Many teachers are perpetually on edge over the unpredictable nature of some pupils' behaviour or academic abilities, for example, so an unpredictable lesson observation is the last thing we need. Generally speaking, people respect – and more importantly trust – transparency. There is something about knowing what's going to happen, even if it's something bad, which makes the process more bearable. As a school leader, your staff will be happier and you will be more trusted if you give the teacher as much information and choice as possible prior to a formal observation. If, however, you are causing them to feel a sense of impending doom, they will more likely be anxious and unhappy and neither of these are conducive to good teaching. Think about it – do you want your teachers to simply comply with you as a leader, or do you want your staff to *believe* in your leadership? Stop the sneak attacks.

3.

Learning walks

Learning walks

Just like observations, learning walks are not inherently bad practice. They can often be supportive in nature, for example where the observer comes in to check up on the behaviour of a particularly notorious class, or they can genuinely be carried out to get a judgement-free snapshot of what's happening in a lesson. No big deal.

However, if you are now working at an academy which has been a local authority run school during your time there, there's a chance you will have seen a massive increase in not-so-supportive learning walks. Oh, and all the money the Headteacher alluded to during the conversion stage? You haven't seen a single penny. You still don't have fans in your room, your blinds are still ripped, and you still don't know who the hell you have to sleep with to get a full set of glue sticks. What you do have, are learning walks. You are being trampled to death by learning walks.

In addition to having too many of them, learning walks are going wrong for very much the same reasons as observations are. Nonetheless, there are some scenarios that are learning walk specific.

WWW: Deception walks

They will arrive at the lesson, possibly unannounced, and perch themselves at the back of the room with a pen and pad. They'll make notes, question pupils, then leave 25 minutes later. They'll then send you an email to arrange your feedback meeting. You've already had every observation you're meant to have so you sit and wonder what just happened. You speak to some of your colleagues and find out that the same thing happened to a handful of them. Then it hits you: you have all just been victims (yes, if you were deceived then you *are* a victim) of an observation. You feel threatened. Victimised.

A malicious school leader may do this to outright bully their teachers, but there are some school leaders who think keeping teachers 'on their toes' is an effective management strategy. However, in reality nothing could be more unfounded. Teachers leave the profession, change schools or go off with stress, often due to excessive scrutiny. Adding a deceptive element to this only serves to worsen the problem.

Generally speaking, learning walks should not be more than 1 to 10 minutes. In any case, their duration should not mirror the duration of an observation. Apart from being grossly unprofessional in my opinion, the bigger problem is the deception itself. As stated earlier, people respect transparency. You know that one abrupt friend we all have who tells us like it is whether we like it or not? We even respect that friend despite them pissing us off every now and again. It's human nature. Lies or other forms deception erode trust and, quite frankly, these types of stunts are exhausting.

EBI: Be honest

Teachers will desperately try to get out of schools where this type of monkey business takes place, so why not just be honest? Set a maximum time limit for learning walks and don't exceed it. It's really that simple. Most teachers are passionate and will go out of their way for you if they trust you so it's probably better that you don't give them reasons not to. On the other side of the coin, some teachers don't object to a longer learning walk, especially if they are about to move on to some particularly engaging activity. If you sense that this may be the case, just ask them if you can stay longer. If they have a good relationship with you, they probably won't object.

WWW: Urine tests

Have you ever a had a urine test where they tell you that if you don't hear from them it's good news? Unfortunately, some school leaders think it's ok to not acknowledge good practice on a learning walk. They walk in, with no discernible emotion, walk out with no discernible emotion. If, however, you're seen sitting at your desk or, heaven forbid, checking an email during your lesson, you'll be sure to hear about it. This is what learning walks have been reduced to – piss tests.

EBI: 'Big up' up good practice

If I was a school leader, the last thing I'd want to be compared to is a urine test. If you see good practice, either acknowledge it on the spot or give some other form of feedback to the teacher. Often, good school leaders will acknowledge good practice in real time by a simple approving head nod or smile, or they may send a short email at the end of the day. Some school leaders even put a 'praise' card in teachers' pigeon holes. Whatever the method, good practice must be acknowledged in learning walks for the same reason as it is in full observations: appreciated teachers are happier teachers and happier teachers are more productive teachers. If the only time you speak to your teachers is when you have to tell them they have type 2 diabetes, they probably won't view you very positively. Big up good practice.

WWW: David Blaine

After a learning walk, some school leaders will send pesky emails to a teacher about how all they saw was the kids 'doing a worksheet' - which, by the way, is a perfectly acceptable activity – just because they didn't happen to see anything else in the time they were there. This frustrates the teacher who feels they have been judged on the basis of very little, and the anxiety it causes creates a need to put on a performance during the next learning walk. A teacher who was once given senseless feedback responded with 'Who d'you think I am? David Blaine or summat?' in his thick Brummy accent. Again, something entirely unnecessary (the feedback, not the accent!)

EBI: A sense of proportion

Any feedback, good or bad, must be proportional. While you shouldn't tell a teacher that they are the world's finest just because the kids seemed to be engaged in their lesson, you also cannot (and should not) assume that a teacher who sits at their desk for a few a minutes while the pupils do a worksheet is lazy. If you see excellent practice, you should praise it and if you see overtly bad practice then obviously you have to say something. But for the things which are neither particularly exciting nor inadequate, just stay quiet.

4.

Book scrutinies

Book scrutinies

Those of us who have worked in education long enough will have seen what was once considered to be good practice turn into bad practice, all in a matter of a few years. Take for example, triple marking. It was once the new cool, now it's the old crap (more on this later). As popular wisdom at the time of writing seems to swing firmly against deep marking, I am hoping that this section becomes redundant and the banality of book or marking scrutinies are firmly out of our teaching lives very soon. We can only hope.

WWW: Bad timing

It's as if some school leaders deliberately circumvent common sense. Like they actually sit in their 8.00am meetings, around their big fancy table, deciding what is common sense, and then do the exact opposite. Call me crazy, but if it's the middle of May and you're busting a gut getting your year 11s to pass, then a year 7 book scrutiny would perhaps be a little bit, I don't know...stupid?

When they calendar book scrutinies in, some school leaders fail to see the greater picture. It would seem that either they are so detached from reality that they've lost touch with how busy teachers can get, or they rather selfishly plan the scrutinies to suit the schedule of the checker, not the checked.

EBI: You can't focus on everything

As with observations and for the same reasons, book scrutinies too should be limited and there should be no surprises. In other words, tell teachers exactly what you're doing and when (if you can keep a straight face while you're doing it, tell them why as well).

When calendaring them in then, be mindful of what else is going on at that time. It's bad enough that you think it's ok to have a meeting and parents' evening in the same week, so adding to this with a book scrutiny will create unnecessary and avoidable stress. Also, if you decide that year 11 are the focus, then realise that teachers will be spending a lot of time on revision sessions, finding the right exam questions, contacting parents and, of course, marking. If you decide to bug them with some inane tripe, then both teachers and pupils suffer. By definition, one cannot focus on everything.

WWW: Secret dossiers

Often, you hand your books in for scrutiny and don't hear anything unless you've done something wrong – another urine test. This does not, however, mean that no record of your marking has been kept. In addition to giving verbal feedback, some school leaders record a teacher's marking via a tick or comment sheet that is usually filed away somewhere never to be seen. Not by you at least. In the worst of cases, you'll hear about some mistake you made 7 months ago which is now an 'issue' for your performance management review. Until you discover the secret dossier, you'll sit in the meeting with a look of plain bamboozlement as you wonder how on earth they still remember that you didn't set your year 8s enough homework throughout December.

EBI: Transparency!

It would have been nice if you told us that you wrote it all down in the first place, and even nicer if you weren't so bloody vindictive with your findings. Transparency: it's not difficult.

5.

Behaviour

Behaviour

Behaviour and how to manage it is a permanent bone of contention and I suspect that won't change any time soon. As buck-passing between teachers and school leaders is common in this area, I'd like to share my thoughts on behaviour management, lest blame be appointed unjustly.

As teachers, nothing causes us more dismay than when we hear this, and I know damn well how much I hated it once, but there is *a* link between lesson planning and behaviour.

There, I said it. But please allow me to explain.

Personally, and most probably like you, I believe that a teacher's strongest classroom management tool is relationship building. But as this is elusive and variable, when I work with PGCEs and NQTs I advise them to plan with three things in mind before they even think of anything else: pace, voice and engagement.

Planning for pace

When a new teacher shows me their lesson plan, I praise them for having many short activities, varied in nature. If they have a worksheet or are going to use mini white boards, I ask them when they plan on handing them out as most of the time this is omitted from the plan, obviously. I then advise them that teenagers will latch on to any 'dead time' in the lesson and use it to do what they do best: talk! A smooth transition from one activity to another is essential; the teacher will struggle to get pupils back on task once they're off.

If you're going to show a video, make sure all you have to do is click play: If it's in some folder which you can't remember the name of and you're manically clicking your mouse, well...there will be a price to pay. Most teachers – and indeed most school leaders – accept this as true but occasionally some teachers (wrongly, in my opinion) consider this to be teacher blaming. Also, there is clearly more to a lesson's pace than this, but it is nonetheless a sound example of where a teacher has a high level of control over the outcomes of their lesson.

Use of Voice

When working with new teachers, I advise them on how best to use their voice in order to ensure that pupils are listening and not talking. I insist they use pupils' names. I show them how to emphasise key words, when to say things louder, when to pause and when to be quieter. I tell them how to give concise explanations, and I even advise them how best to throw their voice if the situation dictates. Rarely can teenagers maintain concentration listening to a monotonous voice for 60 minutes, so much of what happens if voice is not used appropriately is down to the teacher and the teaching.

Engaging activities

There is *some* degree of truth to the opinion that pupils are more likely to misbehave if they aren't engaged in the lesson. Proper use of voice and maintaining a good pace all help but, in addition to this, I ask new teachers to try their best to make science relevant to the pupils' daily life, even if it means deviating from the prescribed curriculum for a few minutes. When I teach the composition of air (most of which is nitrogen, by the way), I tell pupils about how liquid nitrogen is used to freeze off verrucas and warts; i may even show them a video. 'Eeeeeee! Sir, that's disgusting!' they'll say. But they won't talk when I'm talking, or less so, at least!

Most teachers and school leaders will agree that any behaviour policy should only be used as a back-up and, as said earlier, relationship building is a teacher's strongest classroom management tool. Nonetheless, all the perfectly planned lessons in the world cannot compensate for a system unsupported by school leaders.

WWW: When in doubt, blame the teacher

Through words, through action or through both, some school leaders blame teachers for poor behaviour. While there is a link as discussed, these school leaders will act as if it is the absolute link, thereby abdicating themselves of any responsibility.

Many secondary schools, for example, have notoriously 'bad' classes. Hardly any of their teachers are able to get them quiet enough to even give an instruction, and as the pupils are indifferent to any consequences, the behaviour policy is essentially redundant. Instead of splitting up the class or increasing the severity of the consequences, some school leaders will pass the buck to the teachers. They will hold meetings after school in which they will dispense strategies on how best to engage the class, what works best with individual pupils and so on. Those teachers then get to spend their evenings planning 'magical' lessons and making and re-making seating plans, while the sickly enthusiastic Assistant Head gets to leave at 4pm. To add insult to injury, the strategies are often ineffective busywork.

Significantly less, but significantly common nonetheless, is when the blame on teachers is outright belligerent. For example, a teacher once lost all control of her class and so sent for the 'on-call' member of SLT. When the Deputy Head arrived, she asked to see the teacher's planner (the school also had the cheek to ask for planning evidence). After she had read it, the Deputy Head looked at her with disdain and said, 'I'm not sure *I'd* behave for that' – in other words, your pupils are misbehaving because your lesson is boring. The Deputy Head calmed the class down and then left, only for the rowdiness to continue shortly afterwards.

Another way some school leaders blame teachers for bad behaviour is by clutching, desperately and pathetically, to the schools most recent Ofsted grade. Teachers will complain that behaviour has taken a nose dive and school leaders will argue 'Well, we got a good from Ofsted.' A clever way to either deny the problem or to turn it around on the teachers. The worst of school leaders will argue that the 'good' from Ofsted was achieved because teachers planned their lessons better during the course of the inspection. But the reality, however, is that during the inspection, previously unseen members of SLT were standing on every corner during lesson changeover and the really naughty pupils were conveniently absent.

EBI: Do something

Often, we teachers do not like to admit if we are struggling with behaviour (generally, or that of a specific class) for the simple reason that we find it embarrassing. There is no worse feeling than standing in front of a class while they constantly talk over you, to the point that you can't even teach the lesson that you spent so long planning. You worry you might lose control and start shouting, and when you finally do, you compound your worrying further by worrying about what neighbouring teachers – who just heard you losing your rag – think of you. It's just not nice and we'd rather not discuss it...to a point. Eventually, however, word gets out: a teacher starts ranting and everyone joins in.

If the general vibe you get from teachers is that behaviour is an issue, then guess what? It probably is, and more importantly, it's not the fault of the teachers. Yes, there are *some* teachers who aren't so good at building relationships, don't have as much presence in the classroom and plan ineffectively, but it is rather insulting and something of beggar's belief to suggest that the reason entire classes are misbehaving is because all their teachers are, well, shit. At schools which insist on spewing such tripe, the following ensues: teachers stop asking for support; misbehaviour in the classroom continues; the Head teacher smugly walks around sporting a big smile as behaviour is 'not an issue'; teachers become disheartened...you know the rest.

So how do you solve the problem? Simple: *do* something. Don't waste teachers' time telling them how *they* should be doing something. Do something yourself. As the purpose of this chapter is not to analyse different behaviour management strategies, whatever you do is up to you, but it must be *you* that does it and it must have a significant impact – so a short chat with a key player in the class just won't cut it. Or, just keep putting it back on the teachers and one day you may just overhear them joke about how you get paid so much for doing so little.

In addition, clutching to an Ofsted grade is futile. You are blinkered if you seriously think staff are going to turn around and admit 'Oh, it must be me that's the problem.' Even if the good grade *wasn't* obtained by doing things you wouldn't normally, you and I both know that the grade is only valid at the time it is given. Good behaviour over a period of two days 7 months ago does not equate to good behaviour today. If you want the respect of your teachers, don't pedal this nonsense. And, even if you insist on blaming teachers, this is one hell of a ridiculous way of doing it.

WWW: You undermine the teacher

While we have emphasised the importance of relationship building with respect to pupil behaviour, some school leaders have an almost overly positive relationship with pupils. So 'positive' that the pupil does not perceive the school leader as an authority figure but rather as a critical friend or an elder sibling. You may consider this outdated, but personally I believe that any senior leader at a school should have a fear factor about them. As a pupil, I was called to the Deputy Head's office many times (once because according to Mrs. Smith, not only was there too much gel in my hair, but my hair style – an 'undercut' styled in a lame attempt to imitate 1996 Peter Andre – was not appropriate for school) and every time my whole life flashed before my eyes. The sweats and shakes would follow the impending sense of doom and the fear of God would hit me even harder than my grandad did when I had to explain to him why I was at home in the middle of a weekday. She was a good teacher; we had a good relationship with her, but we knew there was a line which was never to be crossed. I would *never* have described Mrs. Smith as 'safe.'

The problem with 'safe' senior leaders is two-fold: they are not firm when dealing with misbehaviour and more importantly, they intentionally or unintentionally undermine teachers. For example, a teacher once sent a pupil out of the room for using foul language. When Mr Bloggs (the on-call member of SLT) arrived, the child was asked for their version of events and then was brought back into the classroom. The teacher later received an email saying the pupil was returned as the behaviour policy had not been correctly adhered to. Meanwhile, the pupil sat in the lesson bragging about how 'safe' he thinks Mr. Bloggs is. In this example, it is not important whether or not the behaviour policy was followed correctly by the teacher. Rather, it's the over-ruling of their decision with the knowledge of the pupil that is unacceptable. By all means, speak to the member of staff afterwards if you think they've made a mistake, but is it really that necessary to side with the pupil, effectively undermining the teacher in question?

As well as the above, schools at which this is a problem report outright ludicrousness which, if not laughed at, would be cried about. A pupil was once sent out of the classroom in accordance with a school's behaviour policy.

The teacher later found out that the Headteacher took the pupil to her office and made him a hot chocolate over which they discussed his behaviour – no sanction was given. At another school, a Deputy Head emailed the pupils to tell them they are now allowed to use their phones at break time, before he even bothered to tell, let alone consult, the teachers. After a teacher strike at another school, a Headteacher deemed it fit to email the pupils and tell them indirectly that their striking teachers are less dedicated. Unfortunately, I could go on.

EBI: Change the dynamic

One of the main determinants not only of a school's success, but also of the happiness of its teachers, is the camaraderie between staff. All staff. Let me save you some suspense, the dynamic of SLT + Pupils Vs. Teachers can lead to a failing school. Teachers may tolerate it for a while but will eventually (in extreme cases) take action. Some schools have unfortunately gone through up to 3 Headteachers in just a handful of years due to one blundersome approach to pupil behaviour after another.

In any case, the feeling of being undermined is as bad and as avoidable as the feeling of deception mentioned earlier. Your school's behaviour policy probably doesn't tell SLT to have hot chocolate with unruly pupils or send removed pupils back to their lesson, so stop this desperate attempt to get pupils on side because it just doesn't work like that. If you think a teacher has been excessive, tactfully tell them afterwards. From you, the only impression a pupil should get is that you are there to support the teacher, the teaching, and the learning.

I recall a previous Headteacher of mine regularly using the phrase 'we are in this together' throughout a difficult period for our school. Another Headteacher passionately raised her clenched fist and told us to 'sock-it to 'em' when we got 'the call.' It was funny, and it created a supportive atmosphere, just like another of my former Headteachers who gave us the go ahead to immediately remove any misbehaving year 11 pupils during exam season. She even came and collected them personally. No questions asked. No hot chocolate. Just the isolation booth. You may have mixed opinions on such type of discipline, but in my experience most teachers would rather work at a school that harnesses an ethos of support, over a school with 'safe' senior leaders who blame and undermine teachers in equal measure.

A note to teachers

Guys, every time we use the phrase 'but they behave for me!' a part of every struggling teacher who hears it dies inside. It is totally unhelpful as it again pushes the pendulum of blame back towards the teacher. Often it is also unfounded as kids, like adults, are pack animals so their behaviour changes depending upon who they are with. A child who regularly misbehaves will likely be even naughtier if they are in a class with some of their naughty counterparts. So yes, they may be behaving well for us, but did we take this and other variables into account before we proudly proclaimed it? I'm not so sure. Either way, its better we keep it to ourselves. No one loves a show-off.

6.

Intervention and revision

Intervention and revision

Once upon a time, Mr Smith told his class that if anyone needs extra help, they're free to come and see him on a Wednesday after school. A handful of pupils took him up on the offer and would pop in with a query about something they didn't quite understand the first time. Mr. Smith, with a cup of coffee in his left hand and a board marker in his right, would casually but passionately explain anything they asked. Pupils would leave the session feeling more confident than before, and Mr Smith would go home with a deep sense of satisfaction knowing that he improved his pupils' life chances. After all, that's why he became a teacher.

Oh, how times changed.

Now, in addition to 2 or 3 Saturday intervention sessions per half term, Mr Smith runs at least 2 revision sessions per holiday. His form is also covered once a week when he is deployed to give one-to-one help to 'underachieving' pupils. Oh, and that session he did on Wednesdays? It now has around 30 pupils in, half of whom Mr Smith is made to collect from their last lesson as he is free period 5.

Mr Smith can't help but look for jobs abroad.

WWW: Devious and messy coercion

At some schools, the volume of intervention and revision sessions has reached maniacal levels. In this respect, what some school leaders lack in intelligence they make up for in deviousness: schools like Mr Smith's do not evolve overnight.

It all begins with pressure. Permeating from SLT, teachers just *know* that their pupils *must* achieve their target grades. The message, subliminal or brazen, is 'Do whatever is in your power to do, or else!' Consequently, teachers, or rather the whole school, enters a frenzy. Off the back of this frenzy, a charismatic member of SLT (if there are any) announces that budget is now available to pay staff for Saturday sessions, and they strongly make the point that they are voluntary. Naturally, newer teachers who perhaps value the extra income more than they value the free time are keen to get on board. And why not? It's only 2 or 3 hrs per session and the hourly rate is a good one. At this stage then, it isn't really a problem.

But not for long. After the first few rounds of sessions, in not-so-obvious obvious ways, school leaders will try and encourage more staff to do the same and the number of sessions available – on both Saturdays (paid) and after school (unpaid) – suddenly multiplies. During post-data point meetings for example, HODs may sit with individual teachers and ask them what they're going to do to improve results. They may casually hint that one session isn't enough, or they may argue 'Our kids struggle to revise by themselves.' They may even collar you at break time and make you feel guilty by telling you you're the only one in the department who hasn't signed up for a Saturday session yet. In short, they will do everything shy of outright telling teachers to do out of hours sessions.

Soon enough, what was once casually presented as an opportunity for quick last-minute revision is now an ongoing obligation. Within a matter of probably one academic year, the exception became the norm. Everyone is working like Mr Smith. While a significant portion of staff end up resigning themselves to it, clever staff are forced to tell clever lies. 'Sorry, I can't on the 18th. It's my cousin's wedding,' or 'Sorry, I've got my kids that weekend.' Once a teacher even posted old pictures of some important event on social media as 'proof' that she had plans that couldn't be rearranged. In any case, neither the lies nor the out of hours sessions are sustainable.

Of all the things in education teachers are rightly against, the normalisation of out-of-hours sessions is, in my opinion, the most deplorable. With the profession in crisis, and teachers already working up to 55 hours a week, coercing teachers to do even more hours is morally bankrupt. No doubt, some school leaders will argue, irrespective of the reality on the ground, that any pressure to do out-of-hours sessions is only perceived and staff are free to do as they please. After we roll our eyes, we can't help but think that if they genuinely believe what they're saying, their ignorance is worse than their crime. Denial is not a river in Egypt, so to speak.

And, of course, there may be the odd school where out of hours sessions actually are voluntary, but the burden of proof that they will remain as such lies with those school leaders.

It can get messy

As well as causing pupils negative stress, out of hours sessions can also have the opposite effect of giving pupils a sense of entitlement. When out-of-hours sessions were first introduced, Ms Jones point blank refused, and long before she was ever coerced by SLT, she was actually coerced by her pupils. 'Underachievement', she noticed, was not only in science – her subject – and, as a result, other departments were also running many out of hours sessions. Some of her pupils would approach and ask, or rather demand, that she do the same simply because the maths department were doing it. She tried her best to explain her reasons, but for some, no reason would suffice. For the first time in her career, she felt her dedication being questioned. Being something of a maverick, Ms Jones had lost interest in what school leaders thought of her many years ago, but being doubted by pupils was both unnerving and disheartening.

It didn't stop there. Her HOD and colleagues took notice of her reluctance and some decided to do out of hours sessions for her groups, without any consultation. So now, as well as having to cope with pupils who seemed to doubt her integrity, Ms Jones was being undermined by her own team, some of whom would make passive-aggressive remarks about how they hoped she 'had a good weekend' while they were busy slaving away.

They don't work

As other factors are entirely inseparable, it is not possible to investigate the effect of one factor in isolation on pupils' achievement. For example, let's say Ms. Jones did the sessions and results showed an improvement on the previous year. Ultimately, she was dealing with different pupils with different individual circumstances, so it cannot be said with certainty that the improvement can be attributed to the out of hours sessions (it's funny how when it comes to data all human variables become irrelevant). In any case, the word in the staffroom is that out of hours sessions at best make no marked difference to results and at worst do more harm to the pupils than good.

Since the onslaught of out of hours sessions began, teachers not only report a rise in negative stress amongst pupils, but also report that some pupils now have an attitude to education which is indicative of a strong sense of entitlement. While some pupils suffer with mental health issues (probably because the constant 'intervention' convinces them they aren't good enough) others, perhaps unconsciously, deflect the pressure by placing it back on the teacher: As one teacher put it, they have a 'what can you do for me' attitude to education rather than a 'how can you help me help myself' attitude. Both of which are detrimental. Stressed, anxious pupils probably don't learn so well and teachers of higher and further education often report that the constant 'spoon feeding' of pupils leads to a lack of independent study skills at A-level and beyond.

EBI: The Mr Smith method

Ms. Jones and Mr. Smith are not real people whose names have been changed. Rather, they represent the many teachers who find themselves in such predicaments. Such *avoidable* predicaments: of all the methods by which a teacher's workload can be reduced, getting rid of out-of-hours sessions is by far the easiest.

Non-negotiables

Firstly, if you use this phrase, please stop. It's disparaging to your staff and it doesn't make you look too good either. If you're desperate to continue however, then add 'no out of hours sessions' to the list. Weekends and holidays should be off the table. If it is necessary to provide you with a reason for this, then please do us all a favour and leave the profession. Many thanks.

Instil an ethos

Everyone deep down, even SLT, knows that any achievement is ultimately down to the pupils. In order to make our children less dependent upon us, a change of ethos at perhaps most schools is necessary. I came across the following tweet by Sophie Bartlett (@_MissieBee), a year 6 primary school teacher.

Child: I don't get it!

Me: That's a statement, not a question.

Child: Please can you help me?

Child: I'm stuck on Q4!

Me: That's a statement, not a question.

When a child tells us they 'don't get it', most of us either rush over and explain it to them, or we break the concept down further through questioning. While both of these responses are acceptable, I genuinely believe that if we put more of the onus on pupils to make a greater attempt to understand concepts themselves, they would become better independent learners, and we could go to Dublin for the weekend without feeling guilty. By insisting pupils ask specific questions, we are forcing them – positively of course – to think. No more is the unwillingness thereof better epitomised than when pupils ask for a revision session because they 'don't understand maths' or because 'physics doesn't make sense.' In addition to say, a 'no hands up policy' then, schools should also have an 'ask until I understand' policy. (I'm sure you can think of a better way of phrasing it!)

Do it like Mr Smith

Allow me to state the obvious: teachers love to teach. The only time we would turn away a pupil who came to see us after school is if there was a meeting we had to rush off to or we were swamped with some other bureaucratic task and simply didn't have the time. In the case of the latter, we would of course arrange another time to see the pupil. While weekends and holidays should remain off the table, teacher led intervention and revision are not inherently negative. Rather, a pupil in need of extra help is actually a good indication that they have made an attempt to process what they have learnt. The problem is the aggressive nature of out of hours sessions. Mr Smith was doing it right. He didn't force anyone; he put the onus on the kids to self-diagnose difficulties and he 'only' offered one session a week. Perfectly reasonable for all parties.

By hook or by crook

Notwithstanding, some may rightly argue that Mr Smith's out of hours sessions are better suited to pupils who are more conscientious than most. So what about those who, for whatever reason, are less inclined to take charge of their own learning? Surely some provision must be made for them? Some school leaders use this as a rationale to justify no end of out of hours sessions. On the other hand, school leaders who want an equal level of provision, but would rather their staff not leave the profession after 3 years, are a little bit more sensible in what they do.

One school, for example, cancelled all meetings during exam season and encouraged staff to use the extra time for intervention and revision for all pupils in danger of not achieving their target grades. Any departmental time that may have been needed was be given back as a planning day in the last week of the summer term and anything administrative was sent via email. Weekends and holidays were rightly off the table. By the same token, school leaders, who appreciate that acute stress can seriously impact a teacher's wellbeing, may encourage out of hours sessions, but to ease workload, they allow their staff to peer or self-assess any tests for non-exam groups during exam season.

7.

TLRs

TLRs

Often within a few years of teaching, new teachers look for opportunities to develop their careers further. It may be because they want the next challenge, have a strong desire to make their mark, pursue financial rewards, or because they seek additional responsibility. Many not only survive but also thrive in their chosen role and some deservedly move on to greater leadership positions. Inherently then, the TLR system is not a flawed one: it makes perfect sense to earn more for doing more.

However, it doesn't take long for someone in a TLR position to come to grips with two realities: that there is never enough time given within the school today to complete the extra work, and that the financial compensation for this work is nowhere near sufficient (the latter is particularly true for lower end TLRs). It is usually the passion for the role or the desire for a bigger role that keeps a teacher going. As the intricacies of budgeting and timetabling are outside the scope of this book, suggesting the obvious area for improvement is redundant. Nonetheless, schools vary in the way they manage the aforementioned inevitability.

WWW: TLRRRs

Some school leaders have a total disregard for a teacher's workload once a TLR position is held. TLR holders may find that because 'they're getting paid extra for it, the 'it' either seems to multiply exponentially, or duties that they were never made aware of seem to creep in. They may, for example, find that the number of meetings, intervention sessions and general admin tasks reach *unmanageable* levels, or they may find themselves having to set cover work for absent staff at the drop of a hat. Because they try desperately to maintain something of a work-life balance, some TLR holders feel guilty that their normal teaching duties end up taking a back seat. In some cases, a TLR holder may be forced to do administrative tasks during the odd lesson while the pupils are given book work, and in extreme cases, teachers take note and TLRs are left unapplied for, often right up until a teacher is convinced to do so by a member of SLT.

EBI: There's only one R...

...in TLR (corny, I know, but bear with me). Teachers who are unhappy with their TLRs report that there are too many last minute surprises, or the moment they have finished one task, another task seems to appear as if from nowhere. Putting responsibility after responsibility after responsibility on a teacher – often for a meagre £25 a week after tax – is unacceptable.

A good example of effective management can be drawn from my own experience: some years ago, when I decided to take on extra responsibility, my line manager and I would agree on an action plan at the beginning of a half-term. It spelt out specific tasks, how their impact would be measured, timelines for their completion, and perhaps most importantly, it would state exactly who I would go to for support. I was never once asked to deter from the plan unless I chose to, so surprises were kept to a minimum. In short then, some senior leaders need to be more mindful.

8.

Meetings

Meetings

We sit eagerly awaiting their finish. We give them half our attention as our minds wonder about the 638 other things we must do but can't. For many of us, our concentration spans are probably less than that of our pupils' so as our minds start to drift, we seriously wonder whether or not we're actually cut out for meetings. Bloody meetings: all they do is get in the way.

I'd like to say that meetings are inherently bad practice, but we all know they won't be going away any time soon, and hyperbole aside, it is nice to catch up with and exchange ideas with colleagues.

WWW: Botox meetings

Apart from the lack of refreshments and the all too often didactic approach, there seems to be one global (ok, school wide) problem with meetings.

As they are calendared in prior to the start of the year, there can be a disconnect between the time of the meeting and the needs of teachers and pupils. This results in school leaders, commonly middle leaders, conducting a Botox meeting: an unnecessary meeting to plump out the calendared slot. It may be that the moderation of a test completed several months prior suddenly becomes necessary, or teachers are randomly asked to discuss some obscure topic. The hallmarks of Botox meetings are that there is no agenda sent the night before, and whoever is running the meeting accidentally lets it slip: 'What shall I do in tomorrow's meeting?'

EBI: Be subtle

Refreshments are essential for any meeting – no explanation necessary. And at the end of a long day, we teachers want to relax and will probably drift off if talked at for long periods of time. We understand that it's unavoidable at times, but please, if it is possible for us to discuss...anything, can you let us? If not, just send us the PowerPoint. Many thanks.

Ideally, if there's nothing to meet about then no meeting should take place. But as school leaders are (rightly or wrongly) heavily insistent upon whole school consistency, it is unlikely that they will let the geography department go home at 3.15pm while the maths department continue to lose the will to live until 4.15pm. To solve the problem then, clever middle leaders recognise a Botox meeting, and only occupy some of the time with filler activities. After, they will subtly tell staff to get on with their own planning, marking and so on, though they'll probably insist teachers stay in the meeting room, lest some pesky Assistant Head makes an appearance.

9.

The dictatorship

The dictatorship

The resemblance of some school leaders to some of the worst dictatorships in the world is uncanny. Ok, I'm being hyperbolic, but at some schools there is a culture of totalitarianism. Your opinion is at best ignored, at worst shot-down. They tell you exactly what to do, how to do it and they even watch you do it. If you do it wrong? Well, you'll pay the price.

WWW: The death of middle leaders

One of the characteristic traits of any dictator is their disproportionate amount of power. In extreme cases, senior leaders influence decisions in ways previously unheard of. At one school, for example, the Deputy Head did the timetabling for every individual teacher (even HODs didn't know their timetable until July 20th), and at another the Headteacher did the performance management reviews for the same. Jobs which were once entrusted to middle leaders have in some cases become centralised.

At some schools, they might at as well be called 'middle instruction followers' or 'middle order obeyers.' Middle leaders, who probably once had a vision for how *they* would want their departments to run, are made to sit in meetings where everything from GCSE entries to the colour of exercise books is dictated to them by SLT. Every idea they have is either dismissed outright, or the Headteacher slyly plants the seed of an idea phrasing it in such a way that an unsuspecting middle leader is made to believe it was their own.

Soon enough, middle leaders learn that speaking at meetings is futile, so they sit quietly and obediently like the lapdogs they've been reduced to. They wonder why the orders can't just be emailed over.

EBI: Get over yourself

No teacher ever decided to take a promotion so they could become a robot. Passionate HODs have strong vision and are keen to make their mark, in a good way, for the benefit of the pupils. By dictating to them, not only are you robbing them of their passion, but the more someone is told what to do the less they can do things for themselves. Such a prescriptive approach risks deskilling middle leaders who will likely struggle further down the line if ever they are given independence.

Because they get it from every direction, most of the stress at any school is usually experienced by those in middle management. Much of this is because middle leaders are in effect asked to disguise your ideas as their own. This is difficult particularly when they don't personally support these ideas, so they literally have to sit and lie to their teams.

Again, more unnecessary stress has been created. You got a 'good' for your last Ofsted, so why do you still insist on being a control freak? Why not have an overarching set of principles and let middle leaders comply with them the way they see fit? As long as the things which *have* to be consistent are, then what's the problem? Get over yourself.

WWW: The spies

As dictators know that they are inherently weak (they are rarely supported by their people), they often have a bunch of goons patrolling their streets on the lookout for anyone who even says anything to challenge them. Of course, you wouldn't expect your Deputy Head to stand outside the staffroom with a Kalashnikov, but some SLT have their ways. At schools where leaders fear union activity, for example, they may send one of their troops to union meetings in an attempt to stifle discussion. They know that most teachers won't complain about anything with a member of SLT watching. And if they do dare to? Be assured that they will be dipped head first into the 'bog of eternal stench' *(Labyrinth, 1986).* Some subtler school leaders may keep tabs on union meetings or general staffroom talk in other ways. You know that annoying aspiring Assistant Head...?

EBI: It's not that deep

Yes, you'll stifle public discussion, but be certain that private discussions will resume as normal. In addition to that, fear is only ever a temporary motivator. Eventually, teachers will fight back or leave, in which case you will have a school full of revolving supply teachers or teachers who are going to embarrass the crap out of you by balloting for strike action. Did you know that there are lots of outstanding schools in which teachers openly disagree, complain and even moan? As my year 11s say, it's really not that deep. Either take on their concerns using the appropriate channels or leave them be. And if you're *that* worried about the impact that 'negative' teachers may have on other staff, then there is a good chance it is *you* that's the problem, not them.

WWW: The retention crisis

Another trait of dictators is that much of what they purport to do is for the benefit of their people. Behind the lies however, it's all done to protect their regime. It's a bit like when some school leaders say 'We do what's best for the kids'. Yes, it *is* true for most, but there are some who have a lot of explaining to do.

At the time of writing, there are huge teacher shortages in Maths and Science.[8] Schools run by dictators are seemingly indifferent to this fact and the consequent effect on pupils. Let's say a maths teacher finally gets fed up of SLT, for whatever reason, and decides to leave her school. The Headteacher likely *knows* why the teacher is leaving, that the teacher will be potentially be impossible to replace, but does absolutely nothing to try and retain her. Disengaged pupils with revolving supply teachers are chosen over a solid teacher whose only 'issue' is that they are a potential threat to the Supreme Leader.

EBI: One conversation

A science teacher felt that the new marking policy at his school was time consuming, heavily bureaucratic and ineffective. Knowing his value as a teacher of a shortage subject, he applied to a neighbouring school after utilising his networking skills to ascertain that the same wasn't the case there. When he sent the dreaded email to the Headteacher to inform her of the application, he was called into the office almost immediately. She even had his lesson covered. The Headteacher expressed a degree of shock and surprise and then outright asked him why he's applied for a non-TLR position at another school. The teacher, trying desperately hard to lie by claiming that he 'fancies a change,' couldn't keep it up and eventually let his true feelings rip.

As much as we would have loved the Head to have tossed out the marking policy, she didn't. But what she did do was tell the teacher how much she valued him, how much the kids like and respect him and how he would be a big loss to the school. She also told him that as the professional, he is free to decide when it's appropriate to get the pupils to mark their own work, particularly if he's feeling snowed under. She also told him that the marking policy is under review.

He walked away smiling and withdrew his application. It's amazing what just a little bit of flexibility and one conversation can do. If you're genuine when you say that you do 'what's best for the kids' then you'll know that stability is a key determinant of their wellbeing. Don't let teachers leave. Compromise does not make you weak. It makes you sensible.

WWW: The blender

Former Iraqi dictator Saddam Hussein allegedly had a giant blender. Anyone who challenged him would be asked the question 'head or feet?', as in which part of their body did they want to enter the machine first. Most schools may have not moved on to blenders just yet, but the hallmark of a school run by dictators is that of over-punishing.

While they may live to talk about them, some teachers have had experiences that can only really be described as abhorrent. A teacher was once given a verbal warning for having her hands in her pockets during an assembly; another for repeatedly setting homework on the wrong day. Some teachers report being put on a 'support' plan and being hounded out shortly after one bad observation. After a scrutiny, a teacher was once asked to collect his books from the Headteacher's office where three members of SLT were sat staring at him, their body language making it very clear that if the teacher accidentally missed one book again, the blender awaited him. After a learning walk, another teacher was called to the Deputy Head's office because he had his teacher file open at the wrong page.

The worst experience I have ever had of being over-punished by a dictator was as an RQT, in the week following an Ofsted inspection.

I received an email the night before the inspection to casually inform me that I had been chosen for a joint observation by the Deputy Head and the inspector. Not long out of my NQT year, I was then still somewhat insecure about my teaching, very nervous about observations and to top it off, it was my first ever experience of Ofsted. I planned my lesson as best as I possibly could and, because I knew I'd be nervous under observation, I even outright memorised questions and explanations to avoid getting tongue tied. I wrote the plan in detail in my neatest handwriting.

Luckily for me, it was to take place during period 1 with a nice, calm year 8 group. I could get it out the way with and forget about it and my more experienced colleagues told me that Ofsted don't observe the same person twice, so after this the inspection is pretty much over.

I pulled my shoulders back, had *Eye of the Tiger* playing in my head and did what I had to do. The inspector was smiling throughout, but the Deputy Head sat with what appeared to me to be a seemingly agitated expression. I became suspicious.

I thought the lesson went fine. In my mind it was a solid 'satisfactory', which at the time actually meant satisfactory. Now of course, it means you get your ass handed to you every week by the annoying Assistant Head who's desperate to prove they're 'making an impact'. Anyway, when I got called in for my feedback, both the inspector and they Deputy Head sat smiling. They thanked me for allowing them to observe my lesson (like I had a choice?) and they gave me the feedback, all of which I agreed with. It was indeed a satisfactory lesson. I walked away relieved, but – and I hope my memory isn't playing games with me – something inside me told me 'this isn't over yet'.

A few days after the inspection, I was casually chatting with me HOD after a morning briefing. We were approached by the Deputy Head, who without any explanation told us to wait in room 28 at break time. We both looked at each other in confusion, each silently

71

questioning what the other person might know about it. My HOD didn't know, but I did. I just couldn't pin point exactly what it was. As asked, we went to room 28 at break time and waited. The Deputy Head finally showed up and said, 'I just wanted to talk about Omar's observation.' Perplexed, my HOD and I looked at one another. 'Erm...Ok' I replied.

The Deputy Head then pulled out my lesson plan from the observation and slammed it on the desk. All I heard after that was how badly I had embarrassed the school, how much of a disappointment I was and a whole myriad of other things. Confused, as only three days ago they gave me a satisfactory, I asked what exactly the problem was. The Deputy Head then pointed to my lesson plan: 'Look! It is unacceptable to write a lesson plan for Ofsted with a pen. It's a mess!'

Clearly, my neatest handwriting wasn't neat enough. I was way past confused at this point so I replied, 'I didn't know we had to type them out.' And then – this is the best bit – the Deputy Head walked forward, not *quite* enough to invade my personal space, pointed in my face and aggressively said 'Don't. Give. Me. That.' I'm not going to lie, I was bricking it throughout this entire ordeal, but you can't listen to Dr. Dre all your life and let someone step to you, right? Instinctively then, with no conscious thought, I squared up right back. In the middle of the school day, in a classroom, I thought I was in a position where I'd have to fight a fellow colleague.

I'd like to say this was the end of it. Nothing further took place and there was obviously no fight, but the sad fact is that the after feeling stayed with me for a long time. What bothers me the most is that it wasn't even a bad experience with a hidden benefit. Let's assume, for example, that I was squared up to because my lesson was bad, it's obviously not right, but I at least *might* have learnt something from it. Instead, I suffered sleepless nights for writing a lesson plan with a fucking pen.

EBI: Be reasonable

Despite the mountains of evidence to the contrary, we teachers are perpetually haunted by the feeling that we are never good enough. We think. We reflect. We feel guilty when it could have gone better. Like recently when I accidentally taught the wrong lesson to my year 10s. Bless them, they didn't say anything for 45 minutes despite me repeatedly reprimanding them for not having any prior knowledge. Afterwards, they laughed at me for my guilt-induced profuse apology and laughed at me even more when I asked them to stick the pages of their books together. So it wouldn't be visible in a book scrutiny, of course. Had I been caught, there'd have been no consequence, but if you can hide your mistakes, then why not, eh?

The point is that self-motivated teachers – which is probably most of the entire workforce – are their own worst critics. Why would you punish someone who punishes themselves? Yes, any form of punishment for writing a lesson plan in pen is ridiculous, but over-punishing for the bigger things is equally as detrimental to a teacher's confidence and wellbeing. No child has ever suffered as a result of a leader not seeing a seating plan during a learning walk. Be reasonable.

WWW: Selfish decisions

If you look at Robert Mugabe's house and look at the living conditions of his people, it won't take you long to conclude that Mugabe looks out for Mugabe. In addition to the snazzy office with the flat screen TVs (one isn't enough), the £1000 tropical fish tank and the £20,000 marble table, some school leaders make decisions that best suit themselves, sometimes at the cost of their staff.

This can be the case when it comes to monitoring teachers. For example, at one school all teachers were asked to show evidence of lesson planning. This is bad enough in itself, but to add insult to injury, SLT decided that showing the relevant pages in teacher planners upon request was insufficient, and so teachers were made to type their plans on to a centralised system which could easily be checked. In addition to this added scrutiny, teachers had to type up their written notes too, thereby wasting time duplicating information – all for the benefit of the checker. SLT tried to argue that teachers should write the plans directly on to the system, but we all know that a teacher's planner contains lots of arrows, folded pages, lists, scribbles and so on, all of which are seemingly random but very necessary. It simply wasn't feasible to plan directly on to the system but the duplication was still insisted upon.

EBI: It's not about you

One of the reasons teachers leave the profession is due to excessive monitoring. To increase teachers' workload in order to make monitoring easier for you then, is doubly unjustifiable. Unless absolutely unavoidable, don't insist on the same information being put in more than one place. In the previous example (and while I absolutely do not approve of checking the lesson plans of qualified teachers), all SLT had to do was ask HODs to glance at teachers' planners during a departmental meeting.

WWW: Good cop, bad cop

Have you ever noticed how when dictators send their ambassadors to other countries, they send some huggable teddy bear who seems to not know very much about the situation? Some school leaders are no different. They will turn a blind eye to, ignore, or quietly condone some of the behaviours of other school leaders. A teacher was once humiliated by her HOD who saw it fit to shout at her in the corridor after school one evening. As the HOD wasn't the slightest bit apologetic, the teacher complained to the Deputy Head, whose response was 'I wouldn't worry about it. He's just a perfectionist. I'll have a word with him'. The teacher later found out that this is something the HOD did periodically and the Headteacher ignored. Allegedly, the results of that department had increased since that particular HOD started, so he was allowed to manage however he felt best. The ends justified the means: he was allowed to be unprofessional.

EBI: Drop the act

We're on to you. Don't think for a second that you can pull the wool over our eyes. This whole good cop, bad cop shenanigan is as obvious as it is vomitous. That aside, a sure fire way of losing the respect of your staff is through dishonesty. I'd probably work harder for a Head and Deputy Head who both shouted at me at the same time, than I would for an agony aunt Headteacher and a sociopathic Deputy Head.

WWW: Deceptive meetings

Saddam Hussein would probably never send the following email: 'Hi all, sorry for the all staff email but could the following year 11 form tutors please come to the sports hall after school so I can put them in my new blender? Many thanks.' Of course not! Both Saddam and some school leaders enjoy keeping people on their toes by creating a sense of uncertainty.

A Headteacher may send a casual email asking a teacher to stop by at lunch time for a quick chat. The unsuspecting member of staff does as the email asks but when he enters the Head's office, he wonders what on earth the Head's secretary and finance manager are doing there. The 'quick chat' suddenly turns into a minuted meeting. He thought the meeting was going to be about the risk assessment for his rugby club, but he finds himself having to explain why he has had three absences this year.

EBI: Transparency!

Enough said.

WWW: 14 different hair styles

Did you know that in North Korea women are forced to choose one of 14 different hair styles, with further stipulations for married women? I didn't either. If some schools leaders had it their way, they'd probably introduce a hairstyle policy alongside their new marking policy on the two boring training days in September.

For some school leaders, if you are not doing it their way, you are doing it wrong. Plain and simple. No more is this evident than during lesson observations. School leaders derive their lesson observation criteria sheet from the guidance given by Ofsted. Mostly, school leaders allow for manoeuvre room, they accept there is more than one thing a teacher can do to achieve the same criteria. Some school leaders, however, believe that their way is the only way, and anything else is at best inferior, or at worst wrong. Take this tweet from #nobservation:

Ian Addison@ianaddison

#nobservation was picked up on the fact that i hadn't used lollysticks to randomly select pupils for questioning and this was bad afl. Next obs i used (blank) sticks and still just asked the children i wanted to ask.

Some school leaders will initiate some practice they believe to be innovative (schools are rarely innovative.

Usually they just take the same thing, change it very slightly and call it something else) and insist it is compulsory. If you don't choose from the set hair style menu, be sure you'll be sentenced to a life of hard labour. Jokes aside, this can be irritating for teachers who have been successful at other schools and are suddenly they are told they're not so good just because they didn't randomly select pupils randomly enough.

EBI: It's none of your business

As a school leader, you obviously must promote whatever you consider to be best practice. But you have to realise that experienced teachers will also have been taught a lot of 'best practice' which may differ from yours. When observing lessons then, focus on the principles rather than the particulars. What's important is that the teacher is doing AfL and that it is working. *How* they do it is none of your business: they can style their hair however they want.

WWW: It's all good

Dictators are rarely known for their moral virtue. Rather, they do whatever they can get away with often at the expense of others. For example, some Headteachers, knowing full well their staff are too scared to complain, will subtly make decisions which will negatively impact unsuspecting teachers. If a complaint *is* made, the Headteacher will feign surprise and usually say something to the effect of 'Well no one's complained to me directly, so I assumed everything was ok'. It is common knowledge at schools, for example, that having a meeting and a parents' evening in the same week is not the done thing. But if no one notices (most likely everyone noticed but didn't have the guts to say anything), then it's all good.

EBI: Have ethics

Consciously or unconsciously, working people imitate their leaders. So if you decide to sneak in extra meetings, expect your staff to sneakily badmouth you in the workload or wellbeing survey during your next Ofsted visit. If you're ethical, however, your staff will respond in kind. Instead of changing the staff calendar and hoping no one notices, why not consult staff beforehand? Just a thought.

WWW: Other 1984-like behaviour

In addition to excessive scrutiny, some school leaders have a bizarre need to monitor teachers when they're not even teaching. Some schools, for example, make their teachers write down the time they enter and leave the building and others make their staff sign paper registers for morning briefings. Some even have absence monitoring procedures which involve you filling in the forms whilst being interrogated by the Head's PA after only one absence.

Those who don't trust can't be trusted.

I can't for the life of me remember where I heard that, but it's so true: distrust breeds distrust. SLTs who feel it necessary to wear bodycams and follow teachers around (ok, they don't do this…yet!) are often viewed by their staff with suspicion. It may be that teachers feel that such school leaders actually *are* trying to catch them out, or teachers may feel that school leaders who create policies for policies sake are blatant careerists: they need to prove they've done something, but nothing needed to be done, so the best they could do was to make sure no one misses briefing. Amazing.

EBI: Professional trust

In addition to the distrust, which is ultimately damaging for you too, having unnecessarily rigorous procedures does nothing but create an oppressive atmosphere in which a teacher's energy is being wasted in anxiety. Do you want positive, smiling teachers in the classroom? Or would you prefer a teacher who's worrying about what will happen to them for forgetting to sign the briefing register?

Teachers don't miss briefings or take days off on purpose (the latter particularly can cause much 'teacher guilt') so why not create a happier school by having some professional trust? At least in these matters? Please? Lots of other schools do and their staff turnover is way lower than yours. Oh, and they're also 'good' schools. Just saying.

10.

Support for NQTs

Support for NQTs

Mr Bloggs' NQT year

As Mr Bloggs was thoroughly enjoying his second school placement, he keenly applied for the post of Teacher of Science when he was not-so-subtly encouraged to do so by his subject mentor. He knew that the school – like any other school – wasn't without its problems, but as he had built strong relationships with teachers and pupils in the short time that he was there, he felt confident that he could take on the challenge. He taught a good lesson, flew through the interview and was delighted when he was offered his first ever teaching job.

Mr Bloggs was overjoyed when he was given a nice, new lab as not having his own had been a constant bug-bear for him as a trainee. To firmly make his mark, Mr Bloggs dedicated a week in the summer holidays to put up display work, and he also got permission from site staff who allowed him to paint the walls. At the end of August, he looked proudly at his black, solar system themed classroom. Life couldn't get any better. He printed off his class lists, made seating plans, and did some long-term planning. He was ready for September.

By the end of the second week, he had taught all his classes at least once. He had a good rapport with some of them as he had taught them as a trainee, and while some seemed to be naturally well disciplined, with others the battle was constant. He could barely introduce his lesson without constantly being interrupted. When one pupil would stop talking another would start, and no behaviour management strategy he had learnt during his training year seemed to work. He was particularly dismayed when a smug teacher proudly proclaimed 'they behave fine in my lesson' when he was letting off steam in the staff room one break time. But he fought on. He would make and remake seating plans, he would reward and sanction pupils and he'd build relationships the same way he did as a trainee. He assuredly told himself 'I got this.'

While his classroom management markedly improved, Mr Bloggs could nonetheless feel the workload mounting. He was coming into school at 7.30am and leaving at 4.30pm only to go home and do another 2 hours of work. In addition, he'd work all day every Sunday. Becoming concerned about his wellbeing and work-life balance, he spoke to his subject mentor (with whom he had a good relationship) who would tell him to prioritise lesson planning and behaviour management. It seemed, however, that different people wanted him to prioritise different things: his HOD was more concerned about marking, while his senior mentor seemed to want NQTs to prioritise their portfolios.

Wanting to be the good teacher he once looked forward to becoming, Mr Bloggs went against the very definition of prioritisation and tried to prioritise everything. Within a matter of weeks, it took its toll. He found himself extremely fatigued during the week, often being in bed as early as 9.00pm. He found himself waking up suddenly in the early hours worrying about arbitrary things, like a homework he forgot to set. He found himself sitting at his desk at the end of the day, lifelessly staring. Had he been of such a disposition, he probably would have cried a few times also.

He bonded with fellow NQTs at his school who he'd meet up with every Friday at the pub. As Sunday was a working day and Saturday was taken by chores and errands, Friday evening was the only time Mr Bloggs really had to unwind. He would work hard all week looking forward to when he and his friends could moan, joke, and most importantly gossip! (Mr. Bloggs probably misunderstood his mentor's advice when he was told to relish small pleasures!)

In the midst of the humour, however, for some NQTs there was a strong sense of disillusionment. Much like the others, Mr Bloggs knew he could do it – he had no doubts about passing the year – but he couldn't help but wonder 'how much longer can I keep this up?'

Allow me to state the obvious: the NQT year will never be easy. Unfortunately though, some school leaders seem to be hell-bent on making it harder than it is.

WWW: The evidence

To the dismay of anyone who's just finished their PGCE, some schools ask their NQTs to complete a large, time-consuming and wholly unnecessary portfolio. It may contain anything from minutes of meetings, to evidencing of teacher standards, and it may even have to contain duplicated information. The tragic comedy is that officially, to pass, all an NQT needs is a signature on one detailed form at the end of each term. It seems that, in some schools, an NQTs workload is therefore deliberately increased, perhaps for no other reason than for the school leader being able to provide evidence of what they do for NQTs. Entirely unnecessary.

EBI: Ditch the paper work

It may be helpful for the NQT to have something in a folder, for example the teacher standards, observation feedback, scheduled meetings or other NQT-specific information, but whether or not a particular teaching standard can be evidenced should be based on the judgement of the mentor alone. If I'm an NQT mentor, for example, I don't need to see examples of marked work in a folder because I would already have seen it during an observation. Unless there is dispute, why create more work? Smart school leaders recognise the difficult nature of the NQT year and prefer their teachers to focus on the bread and butter of teaching. They don't ask for much more than the aforementioned termly form, let alone duplicated information.

WWW: Mr Bloggs was lucky

Schools usually just appoint NQT subject mentors arbitrarily, based to some extent on years of experience. While this is often the right decision, on occasion, an unsuspecting NQT endures a year of disconcert under a mentor who, well, probably shouldn't be mentoring. They may have poor communication or organisation, or they may believe that their way is the only correct way. In the worst of cases, they may be a jealous, belligerent manipulator with an axe to grind.

EBI: Choose the right one

As a first port of call, school leaders should provide training for subject mentors. If it isn't possible, they should call on teachers with strong communication skills and, most importantly, the ability to build relationships. The mentor is the primary go-to for an NQT, and as such much of an NQTs confidence, drive and wellbeing will depend upon their communication with them. When I was an NQT in a very difficult school, it was the relationship I had with my mentor that kept me from leaving the profession or going insane. I still remember him saying 'You may have doubted yourself, but I didn't' when I passed my first term. What a confidence boost that was at the time!

Mentors are commonly not trained but instead pick up the necessary skills from whoever mentored them. It's a bit like how we knew which of our own teachers we wanted to be like when we decided to embark upon teacher training. A mentor is unwittingly showing the mentee how to either be a good mentor, like mine was, or a bad mentor like the one I heard about from an NQT on Twitter last week. A good mentor will create a good mentor, and while a bad mentor may not create a bad mentor, they definitely won't create a happy, confident teacher.

WWW: 'Get involved in as much as you can'

This is probably the stupidest advice a school leader can ever give an NQT. Dear NQTs, if you're reading, do NOT get involved in as much as you can. Focus on your classroom management, lesson planning and marking – in that order. If you have other interests which you would like to bring to your job, then by all means do. But don't go turning up to someone's origami club just because someone 'asks' you for support when you have absolutely no idea how to make a Chihuahua from paper.

The obvious problem with this is that NQTs who act on this advice end up increasing their workload but decreasing the time they spend on what matters. All too often, schools push keen staff to do more, so NQTs end up finding themselves in the tricky position of being asked to do something which they just don't have the time for.

EBI: The classroom is paramount

First and foremost, encourage and support NQTs to get it right *in the classroom*. Anything else, including marking, is secondary. They may be keen to do more, but keen teachers burn out and become resentful when taken advantage of. Organise your own damn trip and encourage someone else to start a stamp collecting club. Oh, and seeing as we're making a list, if you're short a teacher in another subject, could you not pick the non-specialist NQT? Many thanks.

11.

Stand by your union

Stand by your union

The decline in unionisation

Experienced teachers often speak of a decline in the unionisation of schools over the past 20 years. Union solidarity, once a core value of British public sector workers, has faded and been replaced to some extent by apathy and individualism. Teachers (rightly) still use the union when they have an issue requiring individual support, however we have less of a sense of collective identity; we don't care enough about an issue unless it directly affects us. We stand by and do nothing while our SLTs bully our colleagues, and as long as it's not our school that's become toxic, it's not our problem. In short, many teachers no longer see the union as a force for change and sadly, some haven't even bothered to join.

Once upon a time, the majority of staff would be present at union meetings, openly voicing their concerns, and if a mandate for national industrial action was ever passed, all teachers would go on strike. In more recent years however, union meetings are a lot less full and more and more teachers either don't vote in ballots for strike action or choose to go to school despite the motion being passed. In addition, Headteachers often try to keep schools open on strike days by circumventing union regulations – collapsing groups, timetables and so on.

Of course, it's not all bad. Some schools *have* taken local strike action over issues such as workload, bullying, and behaviour, and others have taken 'action short of strike action.' While it is neither a good idea nor necessary to have a trigger-happy approach to strike action, the reason why most schools do not get the changes they want is because of the decline in unionisation: many schools are just not union enough.

WWW: Not quite union enough

Really bad schools have no union presence whatsoever. Through words or action, SLT make it clear that union talk is unacceptable. They may do this through the usual emotional blackmail, for example by looking at you bizarrely and saying 'We do what's best for the kids' when you complain about all the intervention you're doing, or they may hound out teachers who in any way promote union policy, attend union meetings or become union reps. A few days ago a teacher on Twitter told me that two days after a union meeting, all 10 attendees were not-so-coincidentally dropped in on by SLT.

Thankfully, the above is not the norm. Most schools do have union reps who liaise with teachers and regularly meet with the Headteacher to discuss any issues. While the set up is superficially fine, the problem, firstly, is that when a Headteacher is confronted with an issue they may do one of three things: 1: They make a small concession, 2: They defer the issue or it's solution – by asking union reps to get more information from staff, for example, or 3: They deflect the issue – for example they may say the increase in workload is due to policies initiated by middle leaders, so union reps should speak to them instead.

The shenanigan concludes with no major change being made and teachers moaning at the union reps for not putting up enough of a fight.

EBI: A union is only as strong as its members

While the odd school may have a ruthlessly uncompromising union rep, at most schools all-out union militancy has gone. Personally, I don't think this is necessarily a bad thing as I believe that the ever-circumvented notion of common sense is what teachers should be fighting for, rather than fighting for principle or policy (not that these are to be ignored, of course).

In any situation where people are trying to win their demands, the question will ultimately be asked: what are you going to do about it? The reason we don't see common sense prevail is because Headteachers at not-so-unionised schools know deep down the answer is… nothing. They may make a small concession to appear reasonable, but if they defer or deflect an issue, you can guarantee it is because they know that staff will eventually run out of time and energy and will eventually lose heart. So nothing really changes.

As fun as it would be, it would probably not be feasible or reasonable for us to go on strike every time our SLTs did something to piss us off. With the right finesse, however, union action can be both efficient and effective. Take the story of a union rep (let's call him 'Bob' to protect his privacy) that I knew a few years ago.

Bob was an excellent teacher who had positive relationships with pupils, teachers and SLT. He was an active union rep who held regular meetings with teachers and would report any issues to the Head. In most instances, SLT were somewhere between submissive and defiant to teachers' requests so compromises were often reached. Union meetings had a good turn out and teachers spoke openly, free from fear, about any issues they had. In essence, the dynamic at Bob's school was mostly good.

One day the Headteacher announced that instead of having 5 x 1 hour lessons a day, from September the school would switch to 3 x 100 minute lessons a day. To cut a long story short, the Head tried to argue his decision by giving various case studies, research and so on, but staff remained vehemently opposed. As pupils' behaviour was an ongoing issue at the school, staff insisted that keeping pupils in the same room for even longer periods of time would likely make it worse.

During the consultation period, Bob saw the union meetings getting bigger. In addition to the impact on behaviour, lesson planning and curriculum organisation, staff also felt that what the Head referred to as a 'consultation' was anything but. It seemed that the decision had been made and the consultation was a mere formality. Some even accused SLT of being lazy, because it was clear that they didn't want to monitor behaviour during lesson changeover, so this was their attempt at decreasing the amount of time pupils spent in corridors. The 'research' and 'evidence' they used to defend their decision was therefore perceived as a farce.

Being sharp-witted, Bob noticed that the feeling amongst staff was a strong one. To get it in writing, Bob, at the advice of the local union office, distributed a survey to staff asking them which model of the school day they prefer. Not at all to his surprise, almost no one chose 3 x 100 minute lessons. He presented his findings to the Headteacher who wouldn't budge: it was crystal clear that this was not a consultation.

After exhausting every avenue, Bob called what would be the final union meeting on this matter. In a way typical of Bob, he got straight to the point: 'Who is willing to take action over this?' – He didn't specify strike action; union action was sufficient as you will see. Around a third of the teachers raised their hands – 15 in total. Knowing he had asked a question with huge implications, Bob was hesitant to inform the Headteacher. What if teachers changed their minds about taking action? What if the Head got annoyed that he even asked them? Instead, he waited.

A few days later, without even a prior meeting with Bob, the Headteacher casually said in a morning briefing that the 100 minute lessons would not be going ahead in September. He followed this with some long winded, elusive explanation of how the school would look into it in future as part of its long term strategy, but that it was not the best thing for the pupils at that moment. Sure.

In other words, Bob won. The teachers won. Apparently someone snitched to SLT about Bob's little indicative ballot so in trying to save face, they perhaps chose not to hear it from him and backed down before they were made to back down.

Lessons from Bob

Reps and meetings

Bob regularly met with his members and SLT, so his school was unionised well before any direct action became necessary. If you are a good, well established teacher and your school doesn't have a rep, why not become one? If however you're struggling, you risk being seen as someone with a personal agenda, but if you're on top of your game and you have positive relationships with fellow teachers and SLT, then you're probably a good candidate for a union rep.

If it's just not for you or you already have union reps, then it is up to you to ensure that regular (half-termly) meetings are taking place and that you are attending. Of course, the last thing we want is more meetings, but it is up to the reps to conduct them at a time convenient to most members. Staff generally tend to favour lunch time, but there is absolutely no reason why they can't be conducted on Fridays after school at the pub. In fact, that's a good way to keep SLT out!

You decide what's unreasonable

There was no union guideline being violated, at least not directly, at Bob's school. Staff just *knew* the proposed changes were unreasonable. This is important because it is not uncommon for a school defend their actions by referring to union guidelines or other schools. 'Well other schools do random book scrutinies every week!' they may argue, when you complain about the frequency of book scrutinies. What Bob and his colleagues did could easily be done at a school where teachers consider the frequency of learning walks to be excessive or the marking policy onerous.

Choose your battle

While Bob and his colleagues were tough, they were not aggressive. They weren't itching to go on strike to show the Headteacher not to mess with them, but neither were they going to put up with a decision which was obviously ridiculous. They chose a battle behind which they could all unite. Although for them, it was probably the other way round: the battle was the product of their collective opposition.

If any change is to be made via union action, it has to be over a specific issue that is of serious concern to the majority of staff. Again, you get to decide what's serious, but it has to be serious to everyone and feelings have to be strong enough. Unfortunately, too many of us have resigned ourselves to late evenings of bureaucratic tasks so we no longer regard them as a serious concern – just part of the daily grind. Meanwhile, more forward-thinking schools are actively trying to reduce them.

Have resilience

No matter how much SLT argued their case, teachers at Bob's school did not give up. They were resolute and did not simply resign themselves to the Headteacher's decision with the all-too-often-used phrase 'It is what it is.' Instead, they showed that actually it really isn't. If we want to see some real change at our schools, we have to battle through the token gestures, the deferring and deflecting, and make sure our (very reasonable) demands are met.

Don't make a threat you can't carry out

It's worth noting here that Bob did plan to tell the Head that 15 teachers were willing to take action. He would not, however, have told him *which* 15. With this and with anything else mentioned in union meetings, anonymity is assured. In addition, the staff who said they were willing to take action, were indeed willing to take action. If we want to see positive change at our schools, we cannot risk having our bluff called.

Moan . . . then act

As mentioned earlier, teachers will often moan to their union reps but will not be willing to back them up when push comes to shove. If Bob didn't have the support he had from his colleagues, it would have been foolish of him to spend so much of his time and energy trying to change the Headteacher's mind. Don't get me wrong, moaning, along with queuing and gossiping, are core British values (as far as I'm concerned) and a bloody good moan is often necessary! The problem is that SLTs usually know that moaning usually subsides and staff just get on with it in the end. Unless of course if we back up our union reps.

For example's sake, I chose to hone in on one particular event at one particular school, but nonetheless, it is simply a fact that unionised schools put up with a lot less shit than their non-unionised counterparts. The differences can be dramatic: some schools conduct weekly book scrutinies, while at other schools, SLTs cannot so much as conduct a learning walk without a full staff consultation. Some schools still have onerous marking policies, while at other schools teachers only mark tests and everything else is self-assessed. The list could go on.

A note on national strike action

Once a mandate for strike action has been passed, we all know that individual teachers are in no way obliged to go on strike and so many choose not to. They may have a conscientious objection (children missing school), they may see it as ineffective, or they may risk struggling financially if they lose a day's salary. Personally, I believe, perhaps contentiously, that once a mandate for strike action has been passed, it should not be optional, but rather it should be obligatory. I believe that the potential for change is greater if we all adopt a holistic approach to union solidarity which transcends the boundaries of our individual schools.

As said earlier, many Headteachers, for whatever reason, insist on keeping their schools open, despite many of their teachers being on strike, by circumventing union guidelines. School leaders and aspiring school leaders should know that this is undermining the teachers who are fighting the cause, dividing the profession and making us all look rather foolish to the public: teachers trying to shut down schools with Headteachers trying to open them? It's ridiculous!

SLT will normally sweet-talk the union rep for names and numbers so they can make a contingency plan to stay open on the strike day. For striking teachers, a good way to circumvent the circumvention is to *not* tell your SLT that you are going on strike until the very last minute, thereby not giving them the time to make a plan. If asked by anyone other than the union rep, say 'I haven't decided yet.' A good union rep will then tell SLT they're unsure how many are striking, if asked.

12.

Wellbeing matters

Wellbeing matters

Negative stress

As discussed earlier, it is no secret that stress – negative stress that is – is a significant issue for teachers up and down the country. The unique problem with teacher stress is that because of the nature of the job, it can spiral out of control perhaps quicker than for people in other professions. Take for example some of the symptoms of negative stress: forgetfulness, inability to concentrate, memory problems, mood swings, difficulty in making decisions, lack of energy, and emotional outbursts. It would appear that negative stress directly assaults the very faculties needed for teaching. If you're very lucky, you've never been there, but many a teacher have. A series of very close marking deadlines can lead to you working many hours on evening and weekends. Reports are then due in shortly afterwards. You miss the 'effort' column on one report. You receive an abrupt email with 5 members of SLT copied into it reminding you of the importance of data deadlines (and 'effort' columns). You lose sleep worrying about the email. You become snappy with you year 9s the next day. You have a to send a pupil out. The Head of Year questions your decision. You worry even more now that you've done two things wrong in the same week. You then get told your PM observation is on Monday. Your mental health starts to spiral.

While we'd all love a target and deadline free world, we become demotivated when we aren't challenged. Some stress then is necessary for optimal performance. The problem is that the overwhelming nature of negative stress is dangerously counterproductive to good teaching: stress makes you worse at your job, which leads to more stress, which makes you...

Wellbeing

Wellbeing can be defined as the 'state of being healthy or happy.' As the presence or absence of negative stress is a key factor in determining a teacher's wellbeing, school leaders have an obligation to promote this as well as working to reduce negative stress. The problem is that too many are either not doing it or doing it wrong.

WWW: Voluntary ignorance and token gestures

The tragic comedy of teacher's stress and wellbeing is that while it is an issue constantly mentioned in popular media, social media and union conferences, it is outright ignored by some school leaders. Good school leaders will say things like 'We need to make this more manageable for staff' or 'We need to be mindful of workload'. Whereas not-so-good ones will treat teacher stress and wellbeing in one of two ways: they will either deny the problem by not talking about it, or, if an individual expresses a concern, they will be treated as if it is *their* problem. In the case of the latter, some school leaders operate very cleverly. They create an atmosphere where teachers are too fearful to complain about anything so most teachers just end up suffering in silence. If, however, a teacher does speak up, they are treated as the odd one out despite being anything but. They may be passive-aggressively told 'No one else has complained' or they may hear infamous phrase that ends any conversation on teacher wellbeing 'We do what's best for the kids.'

Rather than ignoring staff wellbeing, some school leaders choose to pay it just enough attention to tick the wellbeing box. There will be never be so much as a mention of reduction in workload throughout the year, but on the last week of term there will be a yoga or salsa class because staff wellbeing suddenly becomes a high priority. (The irony being that many teachers will actually see said session as a hindrance to their to-do list and therefore detrimental to their wellbeing). While such sessions are a good idea in theory – anyone who does yoga will tell you it does wonders for their wellbeing – when done in a tokenistic way, they can actually cause resentment in teachers. They can be seen as a justification for an unreasonable workload.

To digress slightly, I believe the current discourse on wellbeing is disproportionately focused on what an individual can do to improve their own. Yes, it is absolutely necessary for us to eat right, sleep right, exercise, reduce our social media time and have meaningful relationships, but it is also important for us to make a conscious effort not to adversely affect the wellbeing of *others.* In other words, I very much enjoy my weekly parkrun, but if the only reason I'm doing it is to combat negative stress, then it is as necessary for the causer of that stress to stop bothering me as it is for me to do the park run. Make sense?

EBI: Time, Job ads, and novel events

As well as following the advice in this book so far, school leaders should also approach the issue of wellbeing specifically from all angles.

Time

One of the biggest causes of resentment in teachers is the feeling of not being valued. Schools that appreciate their staff show them that they're valued by acknowledging their hard work through rewards. By far, the best reward for teachers is not the box of chocolates or the acknowledgment in briefing (not that these don't have their place); it is time. Some Headteachers offer a late start to the morning after a parents' evening, and others unexpectedly announce a shorter day on the last day of a half-term. One Headteacher even closed the school for an INSET two days after an Ofsted inspection and staff were told to work from home.

To acknowledge their teachers' long working hours, some Headteachers offer their staff one 'duvet day' – a day off at the teachers choosing – a year. Some give 'marking days' – where the teacher remains in school but off timetable. Other Heads give up to 4 'planning days' a year, where entire departments are off timetable to work collaboratively. Any way that time can be given back to, or not taken from, a teacher will improve wellbeing.

Wellbeing in the job ad

Anyone who's ever looked on the TES for jobs will know that it is common for schools to a) brag about their most recent Ofsted grading and b) convey high expectations from potential applicants. While b) is perfectly acceptable, I find a) contrived and somewhat pretentious. Teachers would unanimously agree that a schools OFSTED grading is not a key determinant of a teacher's happiness, so instead, why not describe exactly what you do to support staff wellbeing? If you offer 'planning days,' say so. If you don't believe in unnecessary bureaucracy, why not talk about it? You don't have to include lots of detail. This will likely improve recruitment for subjects like science and maths where teachers have more choice of schools. In any case, given the known high risk of teachers suffering poor mental health, it is probably better to adopt a 'Here's what we can do for you' approach rather than a 'Look how outstanding we are!' approach.

Make novel events less novel

Most of us went into teaching because just the thought of doing a desk job was soul-destroying. Teaching is – and should be – fun! In my first book, I wrote about a charity boxing match I once had with a colleague, which the pupils and staff absolutely loved. More recently, we (the teachers) were challenged to a basketball match by the pupils, so naturally, we didn't back down. I can honestly say it was the highlight of my year. Kids were surprised that I could even play (because science teachers aren't meant to be good at sport, right?) and I even managed to get myself politely told off for being 'too competitive.' It was so much fun! There is something about when you and the pupils see each other in different lights that really boosts wellbeing – not just teacher's wellbeing either. In fact, research concurs: I watched the documentary 'Happy' – a scientific study into happiness – on Netflix and one of the neuroscientists recommended aerobic exercise with others and in novel ways to increase wellbeing. Much of the responsibility lies with school leaders in making such novel events less novel.

Invest in a school gym

Yes, budgets are tight, but just as staff wellbeing cannot be ignored, the factors that affect it too cannot be. A teacher's number one reason for not going to the gym, understandably, is lack of time, so naturally an onsite gym will likely increase teachers exercise and improve wellbeing. A school I taught at had gym facilities for pupils which staff were permitted to use out of hours. The equipment was mostly basic, but it was enough to squeeze in a quick workout before going home. It did wonders for my wellbeing and didn't cost the school too much either.

Workload/wellbeing surveys

There are a number of these available from HSE, .GOV.UK and union websites. The sad fact is that most teachers at most schools will answer in the negative to many of the questions on the surveys (one of them asks about the degree to which you have a work-life balance. Ha!) Most school leaders are aware of this, so if they allow the surveys to be distributed it is with great hesitation. It takes a very strong school leader to distribute the survey and then write an action plan based on the findings. Why don't you be one of them?

For teachers

Whether our schools are run by bad school leaders or not, we should support each other's wellbeing and not rely solely on initiatives from school leaders. As there is no end of advice and guidance on wellbeing for the individual, this section will explore the ways in which we can positively influence our colleagues' wellbeing in the school setting and increase staff unity as a result.

Without staff unity, not only is change impossible but we leave ourselves open to attacks from bad – or potentially bad – school leaders. As stated in the previous chapter, unionised schools put up with a lot less nonsense than non-unionised ones but being unionised first requires unity. How do we create unity?

Be the person everyone is happy to see

It is a proven fact that the people we keep in our lives are a significant factor in determining our wellbeing. The person who smiles, brings cake to work, always has something nice or funny to say – that is the person who we should aim to be like. Not the moaner or the 'blocker' who speaks negatively about everything and always looks for reasons as to why something is a bad idea. Keep those types at arm's length. Don't get me wrong, earlier when I said moaning is a key British value, I meant it. A moan every now and again is perfectly fine. But when it becomes constant, it's just draining for the listener (moan *and* act, however, by all means). On the contrary, teachers who never moan are either very pretentious individuals, or they are usually the careerist-sociopath types who will stamp on anyone to get their next promotion. They'll be the ones doing the unannounced 45 minute observations and calling them 'learning walks' in 4 years' time. Avoid them too.

Humour

Allow me to repeat my earlier sentiment: teaching is – and should be – fun! Humour is proven to reduce stress and anxiety so it's up to us to keep up the laughter at work.

Unfortunately, humour is not something I know much about. My colleagues never once convinced me that I was down to lead a meeting and they didn't sit for a full 5 minutes before they burst out laughing and admitted it was a prank. I never once turned all the desks in an NQT's classroom upside down. I never once did the 'floss' at the door of another teacher's classroom whilst he was teaching. I never once collected all the dishes and put them on the HOD's desk after he sent us an email telling us off for not washing up after ourselves. I never once created a WhatsApp group called 'science men' to organise a night out. The women in the department never created a retaliatory group called Organisation Against Science Men- ORGASM. SLT never hired a mini bus to take them to the Christmas do and I didn't sneak on to it and decorate it with learning maps and thinking hats. The Assistant Head did not ring me at midnight to tell me that he's going to observe my lesson on the first day back as a punishment.

The outstanding schools are not the ones that are 'outstanding.' Outstanding schools are the ones with the most laughter. Whatever you have to do have fun, do it!

Whole school spirit

Schools at which whole school staff camaraderie is apparent, are seemingly more fun to work at, and also deal better with internal and external pressures. At departmentalised or 'cliquey' schools, bad decisions by school leaders often go unchecked for the simple reason that staff don't liaise long enough to exchange ideas. For many, it is understandably more comfortable to spend time with the familiar faces of our department, but we should also make an effort with colleagues from that of others, because ultimately, their problems are our problems and vice versa. To help with this, did you know that contrary to popular belief, familiarity *doesn't* breed contempt? It's actually the opposite: the more time you spend with someone, the more you like them (as long as your first experience of them was not a negative one!). We are naturally inclined to best protect the interests of those we like, so for the sake of whole school spirit, why not get out the house a bit?

Marking club

Yes. It's as exciting as it sounds. A few years ago, along with two others, I decided to designate Thursday evenings to 'marking club.' One of us would provide entirely unhealthy refreshments and we'd sit in a classroom (my classroom – I shouldn't have to move, it was my idea!) and yes, you guessed it – marked books until the caretaker kicked us out. The team ethos and refreshments made the whole process much more bearable, and a kind of solidarity with each other meant that we got more done that we would have individually.

You may say I need to get a life, but I can't help but remember it being fun. What could you do at your school to make the boring tasks less boring?

Bring back the staffroom

Depending on your level of experience you may have noticed two things: firstly, that an increasing number of schools no longer have a main staff room, and secondly that the number of people who go to the staff room (if there is one) has greatly decreased. Most schools have departmental staffrooms to which teachers confine themselves through choice or by default.

A cynical part of me doesn't accept this as a coincidence, but rather as a deliberate 'divide and rule' strategy. The demise of the staffroom is common at schools run by bad SLTs who know that if staff talk, they'll unite. If they unite, they can fight for change. But of course, they can't *say* this, so instead they'll just give the teachers some crap about how the school's desperate for extra space. Next thing you know, what was once your staffroom has builders in it for the next 8 months, converting it into God knows what, and you have to sit in your classroom at break making your RBF because you never see your BFF from business studies anymore.

It's no wonder that the interactions mentioned earlier aren't taking place frequently enough, as there is increasingly less space to for them to take place in! Teachers (and school leaders who want to be trusted) should push for a staff room if staff unity is to be an integral part of the school. Teachers likely give up on the main staff room because it's too far from their classroom, they're too busy at break or lunch time anyway, or because they'd rather be with the familiar people of their department. This is all perfectly reasonable, but by never going to the main staffroom not only do we never get a chance to develop whole school unity, but we also put our staffroom at risk. If your Headteacher decides to get rid of it, the first reason they will give is that no one really uses it. If true, that will be difficult to argue against. Use and protect teachers' spaces. Get to your main staffroom once a week.

Holier than thou

'He behaves in *my* lesson.'

'How do you have time for stuff like that?'

'Didn't you know that?'

You're struggling with a pupil; they're not. You went away for the weekend; they never have time. You don't know what hybridisation is; they sure as hell do – and they can't wait to tell you.

We all know that one teacher. The one who looks down their nose at their colleagues because they do more work than everyone else. Don't become that teacher. If you already are that teacher then, in the words of Ice Cube, 'Check yo-self'. It's annoying as hell and does nothing for staff unity and morale. Plus, I wonder how much extra work these 'holier than thou' types actually do. Or are they just in the habit of blowing their own trumpet and looking down on others? Hmmm.

Old is gold

Often, older teachers have it tough. If it isn't enough that they fear their Headteacher will get rid of them at the first opportunity because their salary is too high, they also have to deal with being stereotyped as being stuck in their ways and resistant to change. 20+ years in the game and this is their reward. One of the biggest complaints from older teachers, however, is that too many younger staff don't value their experience. To aid their wellbeing and to harness unity, rather than automatically assuming them to be 'blockers', we should seek their wisdom and benefit from their experience by increasing their involvement in decision making processes – when deciding on a new marking policy, for example. If you do encounter older teachers who are jaded somewhat, then the reason is usually not because they're negative whingers, rather it's because they've seen it all before. Often, whatever idea we are told is the new big thing, is usually a repackaged old thing, and even if it genuinely is the next big thing, it won't be long before someone does some research to prove otherwise. At least when older teachers say something's 'a load of bollocks' they can back it up!

Screw unto others before they screw unto you

Your class underperforms. Your HOD blames you. You blame the teacher you share the class with. The teacher you share the class with blames the struggling NQT who had the class last year. SLT blame the HOD for not making sure you closed the gaps in pupils' knowledge.

And on it goes.

A high accountability and sometimes fear-driven system has led to a culture of blame at some schools. Unlike in probably every other country except for the UK and US, blaming the pupils themselves is almost always off the cards. The obvious thing for us to do then is deflect. The responsibility for pupil attainment will be discussed in the next chapter, but as far as staff unity and wellbeing are concerned, we will have neither unless we drop our defensive attitudes and not be so trigger-happy to screw each other over. It's bad enough that some SLT look to blame the teacher as the first port of call, so being defensive against fellow teachers cannot possibly help make for a united school.

13.

Shift happens

Shift happens

I cannot see a time in mine or your lives when the systemic problems of the education system will disappear. Pupils – and consequently teachers – will always be measured and monitoring and accountability are here to stay. In any case, if changes were to take place, they would have to be on a governmental level and are not something you and I can really influence within the school setting.

The way the system is managed, however, is very much in our sphere of influence. The sheer range in variation of school leadership (phone up a few of your old PGCE mates and ask them what their SLT are like, are they happy, and so on) is sufficient to prove that whatever we may think of the system itself, bad school leaders simply do not have to exist.

To protect us from bad or potentially bad school leaders, and to reclaim the profession generally, a major cultural shift is needed. This usually happens gradually and necessitates a change in thought and action of a group of people in order to achieve a goal. The issue of climate change, for example, was at first ignored. After strong campaigning, awareness was raised, and then soon enough, some people started changing their lifestyles. Those who did, often experienced criticism from people who would argue 'What difference can one person really make?'

Funny how future campaigns would stamp out that exact criticism. 'One person can't do everything but everyone can do something' was the slogan I recall from my teenage years. Cut to a decade or so later; you don't have to leave your house to recycle, plastic bags cost 10p, and solar panels are a thing.

Ironically, school leaders have got the cultural shift thing down to a tee. You'll notice that a clever Headteacher, for example, will never increase workload suddenly. Rather, they will increase it gradually over 1 or 2 years until one day you realise that the school that appointed you bears no resemblance to the school you work at. When they encourage out of hours intervention sessions in a seemingly novel way, they know that it's only a matter of time before everyone feels obliged and the exception becomes the norm. When they increase the book scrutiny, they know people won't object to the first increase, so they'll go for another one soon after. No one objects to that one, and so another one follows. In short, the changes are subtle and slow enough to neither be noticed nor objected to.

Essentially, a schools culture is the sum of what it's teachers think, say and do. We all know what we all think – because let's be honest, it's usually what that one ballsy teacher puts his hand up to moan about in meeting says – it's the 'say and do' we need to work on. With the right finesse, we can make shift happen.

A change in language

'It is what it is'

No doubt you will have heard this phrase used many a time by many different teachers at your school. You've probably even used it yourself. It's use is particularly common during busy periods at work – like when there are lots of back-to-back report deadlines or when there seems to be lots of scrutiny in one go. The problem with this and similar phrases is that while they are seemingly innocent and have a nice ring to them, they are actually very loaded. 'It is what it is:' This suggests firstly, that the cause of 'it' is something external which cannot be changed, and secondly that we have no choice but to accept whatever 'it' may be. To be fair to us, we probably use it unwittingly without thinking about it too deeply, but if we are to see a cultural shift, what we say has to begin to resemble what we think. No one says 'it is what it is' when they're happily getting on with their job without being constantly pestered.

What's normal becomes acceptable, so by using the language of acceptance we are, in effect, normalising parts of the profession to our own detriment. A recent 'get into teaching' advert did the same thing by insinuating that an unreasonable workload is justifiable as it's all for the children. Don't get me wrong: If you're an NQT and you're anxious about being observed once per half term, then no one will disagree – it *is* what it is! But if you find yourself being bombarded with unannounced learning walks, and no-notice book scrutinies, then it really isn't.

The good news is that a new normal is within our reach. But first, we need to ditch the old phrases and use some new ones.

'You should never take credit when the crime rate drops, unless you want to take the blame when its rises.'

Cedric Daniels is a middle leader in the Baltimore Police Department in the hit series *The Wire*. He said the above to Bill Rawls, a senior leader, during their weekly compstat (crime data) meeting. In short, Cedric, and other police officials under immense pressure to lower the crime rate, have regular meetings with Rawls who demands to know why it isn't falling and what is being done about it. Not at all like teaching.

When the crime rate does eventually fall, this is what Cedric tells Rawls, quoting it as advice he once received in the early stages of his career. Having perhaps an unhealthy obsession with *The Wire,* earlier this year I adapted the phrase and tweeted:

A wise teacher once said:

'I'm not willing to take credit for good results, because I'm not willing to take the blame for bad results.'

Within an hour, I had to turn off the alerts. It seemed to have really resonated.

Of course, a teacher's teaching is *a* factor in a child's attainment, but it is not *the* factor, and we should not allow ourselves to be treated as such. It will be difficult, but to begin the cultural shift we should try not be overjoyed with the praise we receive for getting a good set of results one year, when we know full well we will lash back at our school leaders if they criticise us for poor results the following year. Much of the origins of bad school leadership can be found in the pressure to achieve good results, so by rightly acting as if we are only a part of this, we can bring our schools a bit more down to earth.

We could outright make the phrase part of our everyday (it's a bit of a mouthful, but still), or we could express it through our collective attitudes. In performance management meetings, we should show an indifference to any outcome which was not fully under our control. Please note that this attitude should only be to the outcome, not the process. In other words, yes, as paid professionals and teachers who care, we should do our best for our pupils, but whether or not it has the desired outcome is out of our control. In addition, when our pupils do achieve, of course we shouldn't be indifferent. We should be happy – for *them*!

'I did the best I could with the time and resources I had available.'

One of the causes of teacher stress is the constant insinuation, and sometimes outright assertion, that whatever we do is either not good enough or just not enough. Pupil progress meetings are loaded with questions telling us that we could've done more or better: 'What else will you do next time?' 'What would you do differently if you were to do it again?' 'What could you have done better?'

Our job has become a bottomless pit of revision, intervention and differentiation.

By using the phrase above, we are making two things crystal clear: firstly, that our time is finite, and secondly that our best is subject to factors outside of our control. In the meetings then, rather than shooting ourselves in the foot by filling in the forms with long lists of things we could have done, we should be as miserly as reasonably possible when answering those questions and instead insist that we did it right the first time. Unlike the previous phrase from *The Wire*, this could be used quite easily on a daily basis and the good thing about it is that just like 'it is what it is' or 'we do what's best for the kids', it too is a good conversation stopper.

'It will only take 10 minutes.'

Anyone who's been teaching any length of time knows that this is hands down the biggest lie told to teachers.

All too often at schools, time is either mentioned deceptively, or it is not mentioned at all. School leaders will say some 'small' add-on task only takes 10 minutes, but reality dictates otherwise. And of course, when you complain that it took you 45 minutes, you get the smug, 'Well it only took *me* 10 minutes' response.

As UK teachers work longer than teachers pretty much anywhere else in the world [9] and are leaving the profession in droves, it makes sense for us to raise the profile of time in our workplaces.

'How long will this take?' is what we should start asking. Whether it's a new marking policy or some add-on task that only takes '10 minutes', school leaders have to know that our time is not limitless and we will fight for it. It doesn't even have to be a bloody fight: the question itself is neither bolshy, nor does it demand anything itself. Rather, just like the other phrases, if enough people start asking then the importance of time will be hopefully be realised.

Flip the script

Despite the teacher recruitment, retention, workload and mental health crises being constantly reported in the media, a lot of schools still choose to keep themselves in a bubble. In other words, conversations about the aforementioned issues are not really being had in the school setting – at least not in the way they should be. This may be because some school leaders have a need to constantly portray the schools successes and strengths irrespective of the reality on the ground, in that they would rather not have their staff discussing anything potentially 'negative' about the school. If no one applies for a position, for example, it won't really be discussed in any detail. If someone's off with stress, yes, most colleagues will show support, but both this and the former situation will not be discussed as part of a wider problem. Talking about something *is* raising awareness and a lack of awareness precludes cultural shift. Forgive the American slang, but we have to flip the script – we have to reverse the situation. When we hear about the mass exodus of teachers from the toxic school around the corner, we should be discussing the details in the staffroom. When we read yet another article about teachers' stress, we should be discussing ways in which schools can work to reduce it. The conversations don't even have to be in some militant 'don't mess with me' sort of way: by simply bringing the discussion of national problems into our individual schools, we are showing that we are part of a larger body who has a shared interest in protecting the profession. And of course, it's much harder to execute bad leadership on clued up staff who (vocally) know exactly what to look out for.

Self-imposed increases in workload

If you want to spend a chunk of the summer holiday doing up your classroom, fair enough. If you decide you want to reward your year 11s with presents bought from your own pocket, it's up to you. If you choose to use personalised stickers when you mark your books, it's your call. No teacher should object to another's passion.

Problems arise, however, when teachers are excessive in areas that have an impact outside of their own classroom. For example, let's assume you've been asked to fill in a document explaining the reasons why Joe Bloggs is 'underachieving' and the support you're going to put into place. Most of us could explain this in 3 succinct bullet points, but there will always be that one teacher who (probably in a bid to prove they're doing as much as they can) writes too much. What follows is that fellow teachers looking at the document assume – with no indication from SLT whatsoever – that they've done too little, so they go back and add more. The result? Everyone's workload increases. The same is the case for out of hours revision and intervention sessions. If in a given department everyone chooses to do one session a week, and one teacher decides to run two, then it won't be long before two is the new norm – whether you like it or not. Teachers who disagree will no doubt argue that they should be free to do as many out-of-hours sessions as they please. While this is understandable, it is only valid if teachers are also free to do as *few* out of hours sessions as they choose to, and we all know that this is seldom the case.

Just like with bureaucratic tasks then, this is an area in which we should not be excessive. Oh, and while we're at it, stop sending whole school emails! Saying 'Sorry for the all staff email' at the start doesn't let you off the hook either. We still have to read it before we delete it!

It's all well and good suggesting phrases and ideas to enable cultural shift, but the fact is that most people will not use them unless other people are using them. And of course, other people won't use them unless... you get the idea.

So the question has to be asked: who goes first?

Become a badass

It is common at schools in which staff have a bit more say, for there to be up to a handful of Badasses. The Badass is an excellent teacher (notice how I didn't use the ever-monopolised term 'outstanding'? The Badass hates Ofsted terminology) who the pupils love, colleagues and leaders respect, and they are the go-to for all things teaching and learning. They have a good sense of humour, take the lead on initiatives and most of all, they have a supportive demeanour.

So why call them a badass? Simple: in addition to the above, the Badass will do whatever is in their power to put a dent in school bureaucracy – they definitely won't stay quiet about the soul-destroying nature of *the* 'Look! Here's me proving that I'm doing my job!' tasks. The Badass can be SLTs worst nightmare. Not only are they difficult to oppose because they're good at their job, but other teachers end up supporting them in their opposition to some leadership decisions. If you're already a badass, you've probably gone even further than adopting some phrases. If you aren't a badass, why not follow one? Or better still, become one and lead the way to cultural shift? Whatever you do, first and foremost make sure you are a good teacher who is already respected by school leaders. Anything less, and you risk walking around with a target on your head.

Monkeys and myths

The 5 monkeys experiment

A researcher puts 5 monkeys in a large cage, at the top of which is a bunch of bananas. The bananas are out of the reach of the monkeys, but underneath the bananas is a ladder. It doesn't take long for the monkeys to spot the ladder and for one to begin climbing. As soon as he does, however, the researcher sprays him and the remaining monkeys with cold water. The monkey immediately jumps off the ladder and all 5 sit in the cage, cold, wet and baffled. Paying heed to temptation, a second monkey climbs the ladder and the researcher douses him and the remaining monkeys with cold water as before. Eventually, a third monkey attempts to climb the ladder, but this time, events change: the remaining monkeys pull him off and begin to beat him.

The researcher then removes one monkey and replaces it with another. As the monkey is new, naturally, he goes for the bananas. The remaining monkeys, again, pull him off and beat him. The researcher then removes another one of the original monkeys and replaces him. Here's where it gets interesting: when the new monkey goes for the bananas, the remaining monkeys, including the monkey who had never been sprayed, begin to beat him. The researcher repeats the experiment, replacing monkey after monkey, until all 5 are new monkeys who *have never been sprayed.* In the end, any monkey that went for the bananas was still beaten and the monkeys eventually stopped climbing the ladder. All of this, despite none of them ever having been sprayed. If monkeys could talk, and we asked them why they're not allowing anyone to go for the bananas, they'd probably say something to the effect of 'This is how we do things around here.' (NB Psychology teachers, I am aware that the 5 monkeys experiment is debated, but if human behaviour is anything to go by, then personally I accept it as true!)

We're all monkeys

The problem is that me, you, and most other teachers, are all monkeys. While some of us are inclined to educational research, the majority of us just do what our leadership teams tell us to do without really questioning the wisdom behind it. That, or we privately question it but do it anyway. Just like the monkeys who've never been sprayed then, we do things because others are doing them and because we've been led to believe that they're the next 'big thing.' Of course, this is by no means a flaw on us: we'd probably love to read more research, but time is a factor and no matter what we research, we all know that if we challenge the status quo, our SLTs will probably spray us with cold water (the 5 monkeys analogy works on so many levels).

The myths

Despite Ofsted's 'myths' document [10] there are still a handful of myths which are, directly or indirectly, being perpetuated by some school leaders. Unlucky teachers even get hit with the double myth whammy: the myth that something is good practice – when in fact it isn't – and the myth that Ofsted want to see that particular practice – when in fact they don't. Educational writer and geography teacher Mark Enser argues that 'Another problem with these "zombie" teaching ideas – the ones that just won't die – is that they make our job so much harder. We are constantly having to fight through conflicting advice and information to try to get to the truth. It makes it harder to sort what is likely to work from what is likely not to.' [11] It just gets exhausting after a while. Mark also comments on the reluctance of school leaders to retract a disproven idea, instead allowing it to fade out leading to further confusion. I couldn't agree more.

One of the main reasons the myths still exist is exactly this: not enough people know that they are myths! If we did, and we were to make them part of staffroom conversation and adopt some more phrases along the lines of 'What impact is this proven to have?' or 'Do Ofsted want to see this?', perhaps we could prevent some school leaders from unnecessarily increasing our workloads and wasting our time and energy with confusion.

Here are some common myths that are still being perpetuated:

Triple marking

Triple or deep marking (where you mark the pupils work, tell them what to do next, they do it, then you go back and mark that) does not work. Sean Harford, HMI National Director for Education, explains 'There is remarkably little high-quality, relevant research evidence to suggest that detailed or extensive marking has any significant impact on pupils' learning.' [12] If that wasn't enough, the current education secretary said 'Because that's what endless data cuts, triple marking, 10 page lesson plans, and, worst of all, Mocksteds are: a distraction from the core purpose of education. And a costly distraction at that.' [13] The tragic comedy in all of this? 3 in 5 teachers are still required to undertake 'frequent deep or triple marking.' [14] Oh, and if this tragic comedy couldn't get more... tragic, according to their myths document '...Ofsted does not expect to see any specific frequency, type or volume of marking and feedback; these are for the school to decide through its assessment policy' In short, teachers are literally wasting several hours a week making their pupils' work look like (in the words of the infamous Mr P) 'a unicorn has defecated a rainbow all over it'. In the same video he argues 'Who are we doing this for?'

It's definitely not the kids. It's definitely not Ofsted. So that only leaves one other party.

Teaching from the front

It's 'too teacher led' they say – when you teach your lesson with nothing but a board marker and your dazzling personality. Kids can't concentrate, they say. They can only retain a small percentage of what they hear, they say. This too, is pure hoopla [15] It's been disproven, and again in their myths document Ofsted state 'Inspectors must not advocate a particular method of planning, teaching or assessment. It is up to schools themselves to determine their practices and for leadership teams to justify these on their own merits rather than by reference to the inspection handbook'. In other words, Ofsted are in agreement with me, you and probably anyone else in the world with common sense: if it works, do it!

Differentiating for learning styles

No doubt, at some point in your teaching career you too learnt about 'multiple intelligences' or 'learning styles.' This is not as gospel as popular wisdom once suggested. Thirty eminent academics, from the worlds of neuroscience, education and psychology, signed a letter to the *The Guardian* in May 2017 claiming that it is '...ineffective, a waste of resources and potentially even damaging as it can lead to a fixed approach that could impair pupils' potential to apply or adapt themselves to different ways of learning.' [16] While most schools have comfortably ditched the VAK learning, the recentness of the article doesn't bode well for a significant number of schools. Insisting that different learning styles be catered for by no means increases workload the way triple marking does, but again, it's the ensuing confusion that is, well, draining. We don't want to be second guessing ourselves the night before an observation because we made the 'mistake' of finding an article disproving our schools 'best practice.'

It is not within the scope of this book to suggest alternative practices in pedagogy – at least not in the detail necessary. Notwithstanding, if we want to prevent unnecessary increases in workload and avoid confusion, we must familiarise ourselves with Ofsted's myths document and have at least a general idea of the latest in educational research. We should then advocate cultural shift by promoting 'best practice' – practice suitable to the teacher as well as the pupil – using the methods described in this and the previous chapter.

14.

Dear schools...

Dear schools...

We've all got a friend who's been off with stress, left their school, or even the profession.

Hell, it might have even been us.

It is no secret that the UK education system is target driven, heavily regulated, highly bureaucratic, and is probably not inherently conducive to a teacher's happiness.

Nonetheless, paradoxically, many teachers are indeed very happy, most probably because of the way they are led. The proof? Well, there are countless examples of teachers who have left mismanaged schools with crushed confidence and deteriorated mental health, only to thrive at another school only months later.

School leaders, do not underestimate the impact of your management strategies: if you're deceptive, your staff won't respect you. If you're distrustful, your staff won't trust you. If you don't build relationships, your staff won't wholeheartedly follow you. Before you entered the world of leadership, you were a teacher. When you decided upon a teaching career, you looked forward to having a positive impact on the lives of young people, not obsessively scrutinising the books of your future colleagues. Don't let external pressures turn you into something that your PGCE self wouldn't recognise.

Teachers, despite some of the destructive external factors, our job is still the best in the world under the right school leaders. Don't work anywhere you are not happy. Leave, or begin the cultural shift, but don't stay and watch your wellbeing deteriorate. You're a keen, dedicated teacher. You don't deserve constant scrutiny. You don't deserve to be shouted at. You don't deserve to be undermined. You don't deserve to be deceived. Life is too short. You deserve to be trusted.

Notes

1. Sally Weale, 'Fifth of teachers plan to leave profession within two years', *The Guardian*, April 16 2019, https://www.theguardian.com/education/2019/apr/16/fifth-of-teachers-plan-to-leave-profession-within-two-years

2. Sally Weale, 'Almost a third of teachers quit state sector within five years of qualifying', *The Guardian*, October 24 2016, https://www.theguardian.com/education/2016/oct/24/almost-third-of-teachers-quit-within-five-years-of-qualifying-figures

3. May Bulman, 'More than half of teachers have been diagnosed with mental health issues, study shows', *Independent,* January 23 2018, https://www.independent.co.uk/news/uk/home-news/uk-teachers-mental-health-diagnose-issues-targets-education-school-pupils-exams-a8174101.html

4. Louise Tickle, 'Every lesson is a battle: Why teachers are lining up to leave', *The Guardian,* April 10 2018, https://www.theguardian.com/education/2018/apr/10/lesson-battle-why-teachers-lining-up-leave

5. Eleanor Busby, 'Four in five teachers bullied in school with some turning to drugs and alcohol to cope', *Independent,* April 18 2019, https://www.independent.co.uk/news/education/education-news/bullying-teachers-alcohol-drugs-self-harm-nasuwt-union-mental-health-managers-education-a8874766.html

6. Victoria Waldersee, 'Don't become a teacher, warn most teachers', *YouGov,* April 15 2019, https://yougov.co.uk/topics/education/articles-reports/2019/04/14/dont-become-teacher-warn-most-teachers

7. Adi Bloom, 'Exclusive: How stress passes from teachers to pupils 'like a contagion', *TES,* March 9 2018, https://www.tes.com/news/exclusive-how-stress-passes-teachers-pupils-contagion

8. Lola Okolosie, 'How not to solve a teacher shortage: pay more for maths and science', *The Guardian,* August 31 2018, https://www.theguardian.com/commentisfree/2018/aug/31/teacher-shortage-maths-science-pay-rise-government

9. Eleanor Busby, 'British teachers work harder than peers in most other countries, study finds',

Independent, November 8 2018, https://www.independent.co.uk/news/education /education-news/british-teachers-uk-global-teacher-status-index-varkey-foundation-workload-pay-a8622561.html

10. Ofsted, 'Ofsted inspections: myths', [updated July 17 2018], https://www.gov.uk/government/publications/sc hool-inspection-handbook-from-september-2015/ofsted-inspections-mythbusting

11. Mark Enser, 'Are you teaching 'zombie' lessons?' *TES,* July 7 2018, https://www.tes.com/news/are-you-teaching-zombie-lessons

12. Elizabeth Aubrey, 'It's official: your school's marking policy is probably wrong', *The Guardian,* November 29 2016, https://www.theguardian.com/teacher-network/2016/nov/29/teacher-schools-marking-policy-students-work

13. Camilla Turner, 'Excessive lesson planning and triple marking should be abandoned, Education Secretary says', *The Telegraph,* March 10 2018, https://www.telegraph.co.uk/education/2018/03 /10/excessive-lesson-planning-triple-marking-should-abandoned-education/

14. Freddie Whittaker, 'Three in five teachers still required to triple mark, survey reveals', *Schools Week,* October 2 2018, https://schoolsweek.co.uk/three-in-five-teachers-still-required-to-triple-mark-survey-reveals/

15. Daniel Willingham, 'Cone of learning or cone of shame', *Daniel Willingham Science and Education Blog,* February 25 2013, http://www.danielwillingham.com/daniel-willingham-science-and-education-blog/cone-of-learning-or-cone-of-shame

16. 'No evidence to back idea of learning styles', The Guardian [letter], March 12 2017, https://www.theguardian.com/education/2017/mar/12/no-evidence-to-back-idea-of-learning-styles

Printed in Great
Britain
by Amazon